# THE
# MULTILINGUAL
# GOD

# THE MULTILINGUAL GOD

## STORIES OF TRANSLATION

### STEVE FORTOSIS

WILLIAM CAREY
LIBRARY

Bible translators are some of God's favorite "hidden heroes." What could please God more than to see his Word made available to people of every tribe and tongue? This great book will give you new insights into how this work is done and increase your respect for Bible translators everywhere. In the grand scheme of fulfilling the Great Commission, I thank God for this book that elevates the work of Bible translation as a critical component that we often overlook.

—HANS FINZEL, PHD
*president and CEO, WorldVenture*

Steve Fortosis has done an impressive job of dealing with Bible translation for lay people. This is a book that reminds me of some of Eugene Nida's popular works. This puts Fortosis into elite company. Bible translators are often the unsung heroes of missionary work and deserve to be highlighted more often as Fortosis has done here. I hope this book will be widely distributed and used to popularize the work of these heroes of the faith.

—CHARLES H. KRAFT, PHD
*professor emeritus of Anthropology and Intercultural Communication, Fuller Theological Seminary*

This well-researched book will open your eyes to the scary and exciting task of Bible translation. And (hopefully), it might even make you get more involved! I remember two Bible translators working with the Uduk tribe in the Sudan telling me how hard it was to translate Jesus' words "let not your heart be troubled" since the Uduk language did not have a specific word for "heart" or "trouble." Their final translation of those words was as follows: "Don't have a shiver in your liver." This humorous example underlines the extremely difficult task of accurate Bible translation. This book opened my eyes even more to the challenges and joys of getting the Bible into the heart language of every ethno-linguistic group on earth.

—GEORGE MURRAY
*former executive director, Bible Christian Union and TEAM*
*former president and current chancellor, Columbia International University*

This book describes multitudes of examples in which Bible translators were able to take Scripture and render it in other languages so that any culture imaginable may clearly understand biblical truth. It is written on a level that both laypeople and experts could appreciate.

—JOHN REID
*senior missionary with TEAM, thirty years in Japan*

There has not been a book for the general Christian public for thirty years or more describing the aspects of the Bible translation task, the fun bits about language, and the snags in translating God's Word into totally unrelated languages. This book hopes to fill that niche and also be of help to translators today in sharing the story of their work with supporters.

—PAUL VOLLRATH
*senior staff member, Summer Institute of Linguistics*

This book takes us behind the curtains and shows us how the amazing story of translating Scriptures has been unfolding. You will be thrilled, encouraged, yes, and even shocked to see what occurs when ordinary men and women engage in this extraordinary task. Fortosis has surveyed this world-wide task showing us the literary, linguistic, and theological complexities of trying to accomplish this task accurately and dynamically.

Translators must find the right words in the receptor language for words and concepts such as God, Holy Spirit, baptism, salvation, forgiveness, love, faith, and hope. Fortosis shows that occasionally these well-intentioned translators inadvertently present to the hearers a foreign Jesus or a religion that horrifies the people. This task, translators discover, is not clean and simple, but rather messy and complex. The translators must incarnate themselves in the language and culture of the people. Otherwise the translations may distort the message, confuse the people, and lead to heterodox rather than orthodox views of God.

—HAROLD E. DOLLAR, PHD
*professor emeritus of Intercultural Studies, Biola University*

*The Multilingual God: Stories of Translation*

Copyright © 2012 Steve Fortosis

All rights reserved. No part of this book may be reproduced, stored in a retrieval system, or transmitted in any form or by any means—electronic, mechanical, photocopy, recording, or otherwise—without prior written permission of the publisher, except brief quotations used in connection with reviews in magazines or newspapers.

All scripture quotations, unless otherwise indicated, are taken from the Holy Bible, New International Version®, NIV®. Copyright ©1973, 1978, 1984, 2011 by Biblica, Inc.™ Used by permission of Zondervan. All rights reserved worldwide. www.zondervan.com

The "NIV" and "New International Version" are trademarks registered in the United States Patent and Trademark Office by Biblica, Inc.™

Scripture quotations marked "NKVJ™" are taken from the New King James Version®, Copyright © 1982 by Thomas Nelson, Inc. Used by permission. All rights reserved.

Scripture quotations marked "NASB" are taken from the Amplified® Bible, Copyright © 1954, 1958, 1962, 1964, 1965, 1987 by The Lockman Foundation Used by permission. (www.Lockman.org)

Published by William Carey Library, an imprint of William Carey Publishing
10 W. Dry Creek Circle
Littleton, CO 80120 | www.missionbooks.org

Melissa Hicks, editor
Brad Koenig, copyeditor
Renee Robitaille, graphic design
Rose Lee-Norman, indexer

William Carey Library is a ministry of Frontier Ventures
Pasadena, CA 91104 | www.frontierventures.org

23 22 21 20 19 Printed for Worldwide Distribution

Library of Congress Cataloging-in-Publication Data

Fortosis, Stephen, 1953-
 The multilingual God : stories of translation / Steve Fortosis.
    p. cm.
 ISBN 978-0-87808-468-5
 1. Bible--Translating--History. 2. Bible--Hermeneutics--History. 3. Bible--Criticism, interpretation, etc.--History. I. Title.
 BS450.F67 2011
 220.5--dc23
                    2011037609

O GREAT CHIEF OF HEAVEN,
You alone are the possessor of strength,
You alone are the possessor of the being and remaining life,
You alone are the possessor of all real thoughts,
With You alone rest all foundation words.
Therefore, we worship You and greet You now;
We are not strong; We know nothing,
Our ears are stopped and we do not know the foundation words.
But despite all this, we have now come to work for You.
Send Your very Spirit into the center of our beings,
So that we may put aside our stupidity.
Show us what we need to know.
May He help the pink-skin man and may
He help us black-skin men so that
Together we may be able to scratch and put
The foundation words of Your Book
Onto these leaves.
Then will Your foundation words rest and come to be
With the ten clans of the Yui people.
These are true words and I say yes.

—*Segments of a prayer by a language helper for the Salt-Yui tribe, New Guinea*[1]

---

[1] John Hefley, *Searchlight on Bible Words* (Grand Rapids: Zondervan, 1972), 169–70.

# Contents

Acknowledgments .................................................................... xi
Introduction .......................................................................... xiii
1. Great Cost, Greater Reward ............................................ 1
2. Tones, Clicks, and Fricatives .......................................... 11
3. Matching Scripture with Culture .................................... 23
4. The Search for God in Every Culture ............................. 35
5. God: Picketing Peg for the Soul ..................................... 51
6. Family Affairs ................................................................. 63
7. And the Father Said, "*Supo*" ......................................... 71
8. The Road of the Quiet Heart ......................................... 81
9. Kingdom Talk ................................................................. 87
10. Heart, Liver, or Intestines? ............................................. 97
11. Being Strong on God .................................................... 103
12. Hold the Ear and Give a Good Stomach ...................... 115
13. Satan, Evil Spirits, and Headless Turkeys .................... 123
14. For Clarity's Sake .......................................................... 133
15. Hard Sayings ................................................................ 147
16. Translators Laugh (at Themselves) Too ....................... 153
Epilogue: The Nuts and the Bolts ....................................... 163
Bibliography ........................................................................ 183
Index .................................................................................... 189
Scripture Index .................................................................... 203

# Acknowledgments

I WOULD LIKE TO THANK TWO PEOPLE in particular without whose assistance this book would never have been published. First, I owe a debt of gratitude to the librarian at the Summer Institute of Linguistics. This book has been a number of years in the making, so I no longer even recall her name or if she still serves in this capacity. But this wonderful lady shipped me multitudes of books that assisted immeasurably in the research required. There is also an expert translator and editor at the Summer Institute of Linguistics named Paul Vollrath. This friend spent many hours reviewing the entire manuscript and making hundreds, maybe even thousands, of suggestions and corrections. As busy as he was, he always took time to explain the true process of Bible translation and help someone who's never worked in the field to write this book. Please give much of the credit for publication to these two remarkable assistants. I owe them a great deal. Finally, the editors at William Carey Library have contributed much toward making this a top-quality, attractive book in every way.

# Introduction

How does one communicate Christ's designation of Herod as a fox in a culture in which a "fox" is a homosexual? How does one translate "Behold, I stand at the door and knock" in a culture that has no doors? How does one explain the Jewish assumption that women with covered faces are prostitutes, when in some cultures it is a female sign of deepest respect and modesty? And how does one explain a crucified Savior in a culture where male weakness is only looked upon with scorn?

Bible translation is a meticulously complex process. It encompasses a world filled with such concepts as: collocational clashes, semantic sets, relevance theory, and matched support propositions. But in this book your eyes will be opened to the fascinating inner world of the translator.

This book is about communication, and the most challenging form of communication is language to language in a way that encompasses all the diversity of the cultures involved. Our planet contains myriads of people groups, and each differs radically from others. Millions of tough man-hours and billions of hard-earned dollars would have been saved if Christians had been content to retain the Bible in only the original Hebrew and Greek and limit its access to a select group. But there is a message we Christians have been instructed to present to the world, and so individuals have traveled to the most remote crannies of the earth in an attempt to get that news to every patch of humanity. This book documents a few of the fascinating ways translators have transcended culture and language.

The chief goal of Bible translators is to render the content of the word of God as completely and clearly as possible in the idioms of a given language or dialect. It's a challenge to which they commit their lives. To do this, they must know the target culture or language intimately. Only in this way can they avoid a translation that is either too woodenly literalistic or too loose and distorted. If linguists legalistically render the Bible word for word from the Greek and Hebrew, in most languages much of the Scripture becomes obscure and confusing. However, if the Word is translated dynamically and idiomatically, it matches the meaning of Scripture in one language to its meaning in another. This book will illustrate how excruciatingly difficult, time consuming, mind gripping, and even amusing this process can be.

I believe when you finish reading this book you will have an added respect for translators and a mounting admiration for a God who has given us a volume that can speak clearly and powerfully to each people group in its own language across the centuries.

The author can be contacted at sfort1222@msn.com with any questions or comments concerning this book.

CHAPTER ONE

# Great Cost, Greater Reward

VENANCIO, A YOUNG OTOMI INDIAN in the arid Mesquital Valley of Mexico, was so poor he could only offer his new wife a cactus hut. But Venancio was also profoundly curious. He consumed any printed matter he could find. One day a traveling salesman sold him a volume called *La Santa Biblia* (The Holy Bible). Painstakingly deciphering the Spanish words, Venancio and his cousin learned enough to decry the witchcraft of their people and declare themselves Christians. Venancio's wife, Isidra, was fearful of becoming a Christian, but then God healed her of serious illness. One day Venancio found her prostrate on their dirt floor, begging the Bible for forgiveness. He told her softly not to pray to the Book but to the God of the Book, and Isidra became a believer.

One day a Bible translator appeared among the Otomis. He was surprised to find a few Christians among the tribe. When he asked Venancio to help him translate the New Testament into his language, Venancio was overjoyed to assist.[2]

It is for this joy that Bible translators are willing to devote their lives to an activity that has been described by some as the most complex intellectual activity in which any person can engage. Translators

---

2 Hefley, *Searchlight on Bible Words*, 26–27.

must not only learn a new language but must learn to speak and write that language, translating thoughts and ideas so that they will be easily understandable to those whose cultural history, practices, and beliefs may be vastly diverse.³ Early priests in Mexico even questioned if it could be done. The Spanish crown stated that "none of the native languages is sufficiently rich or supple enough to allow it to be used for explaining the mysteries of the Christian faith."⁴

The centuries have proven the opposite. One expert linguist states that, in a sense, the Bible is the most translatable religious book ever written, for it comes from the western end of the Fertile Crescent through which passed more cultural patterns and out from which radiated more distinctive features and values than any other place in world history. In fact, comparison of the cultural traits in the Bible with those of all existing cultures (at least two thousand) reveals that the Bible is much closer to *them* than to the technological culture of the Western world.⁵

What does it cost to translate the Bible into another language? It cannot be measured in financial terms or even educational value. It cannot be measured in any tangible way. It costs the very lives of those who volunteer and are trained for such a vast undertaking. Some individuals and couples devote their entire careers—thirty, forty years or more to translating the Bible into the language of, perhaps, less than a thousand people.

Jesus told his disciples that the end would not come until the gospel had reached all nations. India is one nation, but this nation alone contains 3,500 people groups, many of which speak their own unique dialect.⁶ Thus, some scholars believe that the Greek phrase *ta ethne* in Mark 13:10 might rather be rendered "all people groups" rather than "all nations." Scriptures such as this have convinced translators that everyone possible needs to have the words of the Bible, and

---

3 Eugene Nida and Jan de Waard, *From One Language to Another: Functional Equivalence in Bible Translating* (Nashville: Thomas Nelson, 1986), 181.
4 Robert Ricard, *The Spiritual Conquest of Mexico* (Berkeley: University of California Press, 1966), 51.
5 Eugene Nida and William Reyburn, *Meaning across Cultures* (Maryknoll, NY: Orbis Books, 1981), 28.
6 Don Richardson, *Eternity in Their Hearts* (Ventura, CA: Regal Books, 1974), 149.

that the salvation of even one soul is worth a lifetime of meticulous, mind-bending linguistic work.

It is this passion that must evolve into compassion in every translating venture. A genuine reverence for the word of God must go hand in hand with a deep interest in the people. Christ combined the searching "Who do you say that I am?" with the caring "Zaccheus, come down immediately. I must stay at your house today." Biblical teaching in worldwide cultures must not begin with a study of Augustine, Luther, and Calvin, but instead, it must begin with a love for people.

Translation dreams, however, do not always work out as planned. Marianna Slocum and Bill Bentley planned to marry and translate the Bible into the Tzeltal language. Bill had begun the work as a bachelor, but as he headed back to the United States for the wedding, he experienced a fatal heart attack. Instead of enmeshing herself in grief and self-centered goals, Mariana decided to go to the Tzeltals anyway and, with the help of a partner, devoted many years to Bible translation.[7]

W. F. Jordan told a group of tribespeople in La Paz, Bolivia, that, just as the Bible had been translated into Quechua, he hoped it would also be translated into the Aymara language. After his talk, an ancient Aymara man approached him and uttered only one brief sentence: "Your word was very sweet to me," but those words stirred Jordan more than anything he could remember.[8]

However, among receptor cultures there are sometimes contrasting reactions to Bible translators. Eunice Pike writes, "Some wanted to learn to read, others tossed stones while we taught; people wanted our medicine—others called it rat poison; people thanked us for teaching them about Christ—others called us devils; people told us how glad they were that we were in town—others tried to drive us out."[9]

There are situations in which, before work can even begin, strange or terrifying myths about the translators must be dismissed. When

---

7 Hefley, *Searchlight on Bible Words*, 32.
8 W. F. Jordan, *Glimpses of Indian America: Illustrating Present-day Life in Mexico and Parts of Central and South America* (New York: Revell, 1923), 144.
9 Eunice Pike, *An Uttermost Part* (Chicago: Moody Press, 1971), 65.

Leslie and Kitty Pride went to work among the Chatino people of southwest Mexico, one old man was surprised they had survived the trip to Mexico. He said, "There are four seas. The first one by the shore is salt water [the Pacific]. When you get through that, you come to the Mud Sea. Then you go on to the Sea of Blood, and beyond that is the Sea of Pitch, which no one can get through . . . Can a big woodhouse [boat] really go through that pitch?"

The couple had no sooner straightened out that misconception when a little nine-year-old Chatino girl asked, "It isn't true, is it?"

"What isn't true?" asked Kitty.

"That you eat dead children?"

"No, of course not! Whoever said that?"

"You remember that child's funeral yesterday? Someone said you went out to the graveyard last night and dug up the coffin to eat the corpse."[10]

When James Marsh visited the Kunjen people in Australia, he was astounded at the complete vacuum of spiritual knowledge. When the Kunjen men learned Marsh was from the United States, they fired questions such as "Was Billy the Kid a real bloke?" "Have you ever been to the town of Tombstone?" "Do the Apaches still attack stagecoaches?" "Have you seen Boot Hill?" Then they began posing questions like, "Is it really true about Jerusalem and Egypt . . . and what about Jesus? Was he real?" James spoke to them of these faraway places and people. And, he assured them, Jesus was very real and one day they'd learn about him in their own language.[11]

Nationals sometimes sense the importance of Bible translation from the start. When a bright young Navajo man volunteered to be Faye Edgerton's language assistant, she warned him, "You won't make much money helping me . . . we can't pay very much."

"What's money?" he said. "It won't last forever—but this Book will. I want my people to have it."[12]

Assistants are sometimes a bit shocked as they help translate radical new truth for the first time. When Nogo, language assistant in

---

10 Kitty Pride, *Bread Is Not Enough* (London: Hodder & Stoughton, 1976).
11 Hefley, *Searchlight on Bible Words*, 179.
12 Ethel Wallis, *God Speaks Navajo* (New York: Harper & Row, 1968), 94.

the Usarufa language, heard in his language that Jesus told the wind and water to be quiet, he was incredulous. He cried, "No! No! Wind and water don't obey."

Translators thought they'd used the wrong word and began reviewing it with Nogo. Finally he realized that it was true as expressed. Jesus had actually calmed nature's fury with a word. Many times in days to come, Nogo could be heard saying to a fellow tribesman, "Have you heard of how this Jesus made the wind obey?"[13]

Over and over, the power of God through his Word is evident. One day a translator was trying to sell portions of Scripture in a Mexican marketplace. As Indians passed by, she would read aloud some verses of Scripture to attract their interest. A brash, wisecracking drunk joined the little crowd around the table. At the same time, a man touched a Gospel of John and asked, "What does this one say?"

Praying silently that the drunk wouldn't scatter the group, the translator read a few verses from chapter fourteen where Jesus assures his followers that he is going to prepare a place for them. Immediately the drunk stopped his taunting and didn't utter a sound until the Scripture reading was finished. Then he thrust out his hand, "I want that book."

The crowd gasped. Sensing their surprise, the man became embarrassed and fumbled for his money. He paid for the booklet and disappeared quickly into the crowds. The translator never saw him again but found herself praying for the man at odd moments, wondering.[14]

Among some isolated peoples there is a strong desire to learn. One Indian chief traveled a long distance to Plateria, Peru, telling missionaries his village would support a teacher if they would provide one. Told there was no teacher, the chief refused to return home without one. He dug in his heels for ten days until a missionary finally procured a volunteer to go teach these people how to read God's truth.[15]

---

13 Ibid., 52–53.
14 Pike, *An Uttermost Part*, 121.
15 W. Jordan, *Glimpses of Indian America*, 125.

When people finally have God's words in their own language, there is often a hunger for it that is almost palpable. A Mazatec Indian boy was loaned a copy of a Bible story in his own language. This was before the proliferation of word processors and Xerox machines, so translators couldn't give out multiple copies. The next day the boy came back for another story. Finally, he said, "If you have grace [the Mazatec way of saying please] . . . that is, my mother says would you have grace and copy these papers for us? We want them to keep."

Eunice Pike hesitated. She knew that if she kept typing copies of stories for people she'd never get to new translation work.

The boy spoke again. "Have grace, my father says he will pay you." He was not begging—from under his shirt he pulled six new sheets of typing paper he had somehow acquired.

Finally he said, "My father says, if you are too busy, will you give the first stories back again? I will copy them myself."

Very impressed, Pike gave him the Bible stories. The boy would probably spend many hours copying with a stubby old pencil these stories that he and his family had come to recognize as precious.[16]

A young Cree Indian girl was orphaned at age six and then almost starved to death by uncaring relatives. The girl's name was Astumastao, and missionary James Evans rescued her and for a year, taught her Scripture verses, hymns, and choruses.

Then the girl's uncle, Kistayimoowin, came and took the girl as a helper for his wife. Another uncle lived in the same home. He'd been mistreated by whites, and he hated them. Once, when he heard Astumastao singing a chorus, he rushed out of the wigwam and beat her unconscious. He said that the next time he heard a white man's song, he would kill her.

Years passed, Astumastao grew up, and little by little the songs and Scriptures faded. However she still demonstrated subconsciously many of the Christian graces and steadfastly refused to practice the pagan ways of the tribe.

One summer Kistayimoowin went to a certain island where the fishing and hunting were good. He fired his old flintlock at some ducks and it exploded in his hands, blowing one of his hands

---

16 Eunice Pike, *Words Wanted* (Chicago: Moody Press, 1958), 75.

completely off. Astumastao came to his rescue, but the blood loss was great. He went into a stupor. Finally he roused himself and spoke the Cree word for "sing." In a low voice she sang in Cree her favorite Christian song:

> Jesus my all to heaven is gone,
> He whom I fix my hopes upon;
> His track I see and I'll pursue
> The narrow way till him I view.

"Who is this Jesus?" he murmured.

"He is the Son of the Great Spirit—he died to save us. 'For God loved this world so much that he gave his only Son, that whosoever believes in him should not perish but have everlasting life.'"

Her uncle said, "Say it again and again."

She repeated the verse several times.

"Can you remember anything more?"

"I do remember that my teacher taught me that this Jesus said something like, 'Who comes to me I will never cast out.'"

"Did he say that included the Indian?"

"Yes," said the girl, "the good missionary said he loved all."

"Sing again," he said.

> Lo, glad I come and you, blest Lamb,
> Shall take me to you as I am.
> Nothing but sin have I to give,
> Nothing but love shall I receive.

"What did you say was his name?"

"Jesus," she said.

"Lift up my head," he said to his wife. "Take hold of my hand, my niece. It is getting so dark. I cannot see the trail. I have no guide. What did you say was his name?"

"Jesus," she said, sobbing.

And with that name on his lips he was gone.[17]

---

17 Gordon Fraser, *No Dark Valley: A Collection of Stories about Indians and Missions to Indian Tribes* (Flagstaff, AZ: Southwestern School of Missions, 1965), 57–62.

Another Indian, a Mazatec, also heard John 3 and asked a translator, "Is it true we must be born again?"

"Yes, that's what the Bible says."

"What does a person look like who has been born a second time?" he asked.

"It's his heart or soul that looks different. Christ gives him a new heart."

The man was not quite satisfied. "Can even murderers enter heaven?" (Murder was frequent in the region.)

"Yes. Even a murderer, because Christ takes his guilt upon himself. Of course, if a man really believes, he won't commit murder again."

The man sat for a while and began to ponder what heaven would be like.

"Do men plant corn up there?" he inquired.

"The Bible doesn't say," said the translator, "but we will have everything we need."[18]

When the gospel was explained to another Mazatec, he interrupted, "Is that written someplace?"

Eunice Pike handed him a copy of 1 John in Mazatec and Spanish, and the two examined some Scriptures. Finally he was ready to become a Christian. He thought for a minute, then asked, "What language do I talk?"

"You can speak either Mazatec or Spanish. God understands both."

Silence. "What do I call him?"

"Call him Father because now that you believe in Jesus, God is your Father."

So he bowed his head and received Christ into his life.[19]

After a volcano erupted near the Guatemalan village of Santa Maria, the people turned, not to Christ, but to witch doctors to pacify the volcano. With their exorcisms and incantations, the witch doctors were revered like the pope himself.

---

18 Eunice Pike, *Not Alone* (Chicago: Moody Press, 1956), 114.
19 Pike, *An Uttermost Part*, 36.

Amazingly, one witch doctor heard the gospel, became conscience stricken, gave up his vices, and destroyed the cultic paraphernalia. Persecution immediately followed, and he was arrested and sent to work with a road building gang. The ex-witch doctor couldn't keep quiet about his faith, and he began whispering of the subject to his immediate supervisor, Marcelino Velasquez.

In time Velasquez began asking curious questions and, realizing he didn't know enough to answer, the former witch doctor told him to contact missionary Paul Burgess. Velasquez began sneaking the missionary into his home. There Burgess taught him to read the Bible, and eventually he became a devoted Christian. One day when Burgess arrived, Velasquez was radiant. "I've done it! I've done it!" he shouted. "I told them I was a believer."

The day before, the council of chiefs had begun denigrating the missionaries, and Velasquez finally interrupted. "Those things are not true. I am one of them, and I know." Eventually, because of Velasquez's generous giving, one of the most attractive little chapels in the republic was built just outside his hometown.[20]

This book will reveal hundreds of specific examples of how translators have made it possible for individuals such as the ones in this chapter to understand the Bible well enough not only to be converted but to grow toward fuller spiritual maturity. We will discover how complex the process of translation is and how linguists decide exactly what words to use in describing God, faith, love, forgiveness, prayer, and many other concepts. The process will leave you stimulated, awed, and exhilarated. Prepare for a remarkable linguistic journey.

---

20 W. F. Jordan, *Central American Indians and the Bible* (New York: Revell, 1926), 53–57.

CHAPTER TWO

# Tones, Clicks, and Fricatives

B<small>Y THE 1960S, THE BALANGAO TRIBE</small> of the Philippines was not exactly enormous. In the high mountains, several days' hike out of Manila, only about seven thousand Balangaos remained.

Balangaos were headhunters by tradition but, thankfully, the tradition had mostly become a thing of the past. All newcomer Joanne Shetler knew was that they needed their own translation of the Scriptures. In fact, Balangao elders had voted to invite white translators into their culture, and Joanne and a partner had decided to accept the invitation.[21]

Initiation into Balangao language and culture began in 1962 as, day and night, people crowded around Joanne and her partner, trying to teach them words and correcting their pronunciation.[22] The massive task ahead of the women loomed larger and larger as they realized how many words and language traits they must learn.

An elder in the area named Ama became Jo Shetler's self-appointed protector. In fact, with time he began looking upon her as his adopted daughter. He was always there to help her with the many adjustments

---

21 Joanne Shetler, *And the Word Came with Power* (Orlando: Wycliffe Bible Translators, 2000), 32.
22 Ibid., 40.

to a new culture and new surroundings. However, after serving for five years, Shetler had seen only two Balangaos turn from the spirits to the living God, and Ama was not one of them.[23]

Then one night a baby died unexpectedly in a village, and the people began asking Shetler questions: *Why do you pray? What do the prayers mean? Where do we go when we die? What about the resurrection?* She began a Bible study, and attendance gradually grew.[24]

After Shetler had been with the Balangaos for six years, one day Ama opened a New Testament and saw what looked like a list of peoples' names. He asked in effect, "Is this a genealogy of mankind?" Joanne explained that indeed it was a partial list of human descendants, beginning with the first couple, Adam and Eve. Ama was incredulous. "You mean this book has a genealogy in it? You mean this is true? We always thought it was the rock and the banana plant that gave birth to humans. But we never had people's names written down."[25]

The written genealogy was powerful stuff to the Balangaos. They placed great importance on one's descendants. As in some other cultures, genealogies were often recited by memory for the purpose of validating ownership, confirming one's familial claims, or lending credibility by establishing rights.[26] The genealogy which started from the first human proved the Bible was true. No one else knew such information. It was only the next week that Ama brought others with him to Shetler.

"Teach us about that word of God you are translating," he demanded.[27]

Shetler had not yet been able to train others to teach Bible studies on Sundays, so she always did it. Finally Ama rose one Sunday and said, "My daughter knows more about the Book than I do, but we found in the Bible where it says that women aren't supposed to

---

23 Ibid., 77.
24 Ibid., 79–80.
25 Ibid., 81–82.
26 Daniel Shaw, *Transculturation: The Cultural Factor in Translation and Other Communication Tasks* (Pasadena: William Carey Library, 1988), 126.
27 Shetler, *And the Word Came*, 84.

teach men, so I guess I have to be the one." So Ama became the first "pastor/teacher."[28]

As the years passed, Ama wore out three shelf-paper Bible genealogies explaining to all who would listen how they, too, could become a part of God's eternal genealogy.[29]

The Awa people of New Guinea were also very slow to believe the gospel. It took years for Richard and Aretta Loving to translate the Gospel of Mark into the Awa language. At its completion, only one member of the Awas claimed to be a Christian. The Lovings stayed on an extra six months beyond furlough time to complete the translation of 1 John and 2 John so that those who had heard the gospel might have some criteria for knowing when they could actually call themselves true believers.

The Lovings were gratified to learn upon their return a year later that Tobiona and Punuyaba, two translation assistants, had also placed their faith in Christ. In fact, they were spending their evenings going from hut to hut, encouraging the elders of the village to become "really alive."[30]

And this is what it's about. All the years of painstaking work are worth it when translators see the Spirit of God begin drawing people to transformation in Christ. Translating the Bible into a new language does not guarantee that a receptor people will become believers, but they certainly can't be converted and reach maturity in Christ without it. And it is just as Isaiah wrote, God sees that his Word always reaps eternal dividends, and it accomplishes all that God intends among a people (Isa 55:11).

Before a translation team is even formed, leaders must decide whether a target language may actually be extinct before Scripture translation is completed. For example, the Votic language of the Russian coast is only spoken by three hundred and, at this writing, the Oro Sin dialect of Lowland Amazonia has only three speakers left.[31]

---

28 Ibid., 87.
29 Ibid., 136.
30 Hefley, *Searchlight on Bible Words*, 14–17.
31 Harriet Barovick, "Tongues that Go out of Style," *Time*, June 10, 2002, 22.

Of course, translators must identify symbols for thousands of objects and concepts and use them to render a Bible translation that is not unnatural and stilted, but is as lively, vivid, and flowing as the original languages were to ancient Hebrews and Greeks. And the goal is not simply to enable the recipients to understand the basic data of the Bible but to sense its crucial relevance to life and to respond to it in action.

Languages such as Chinese have very complex alphabets. Chinese is built of 214 symbols called radicals, which are combined to form up to fifty thousand ideographs! These ideographs sometimes actually *picture* the meaning of the word they symbolize. For example, Bible translators were amazed when they considered the ideograph for the word "righteous." The upper part of the ideograph was the Chinese symbol for "lamb." The lower part was the symbol for the personal pronoun "I." Thus it pictured: "I under the lamb am righteous." The ideograph for "boat" embodies a boat with eight people in it. Noah's ark contained exactly eight people too. Are these examples and others purely coincidental? It makes one wonder.

Sometimes a Scripture in a receptor language requires fewer words than in English. For example, in the Quiche language of Guatemala, "to watch sheep at night" requires only one word.[32] In other cases, *more* words are required than in English. For instance, "The wages for sin is death" must be expressed, "If a person sins, the pay he will receive for that will cause him to die."[33]

Whether or not Scriptures are concretely presented often depends on the culture. Some of the peoples of Meso-America have languages that are very literal or are intolerant of unfamiliar figures of speech; others welcome figures of speech and take delight in curiously deciphering them. This has nothing to do with intelligence; it's a matter of cultural practice. A translator's first goal is to translate metaphorical ideas literally. If the words won't translate directly, the translator tries using a more acceptable figure of speech. If it still causes confusion, a literal explanation when it is taught may be required.

---

[32] Hugh Coke, *An Ethnohistory of Bible Translation among the Maya* (Ann Arbor: University Microfilms International, 1983), 275.

[33] Eugene Nida, *Bible Translating: An Analysis of Principles and Procedures* (New York: American Bible Society, 1947), 98.

For instance, when the Chols of Mexico read in Mark 14:63 that the high priest "tore his clothes," they thought he had perhaps gone temporarily insane—surely if he was angry with someone he would have torn up *that* person's clothes. Or maybe he'd begun perspiring in the course of the trial and was trying to cool off. In cases like this, many translators believe they should state explicitly why the man tore his clothes.[34]

A related danger for translators is oversimplifying biblical concepts. In the Greek, there are a number of words representing sin: *hamartia* (missing the mark), *adikia* (injustice), *kakia* (malice, evil), *anomia* (lawlessness), etc. However, a temptation in translating Japanese is to narrow sin down to one basic word: *tsumi*. Not only may this oversimplify the concept, it may also not be fully accurate. *Tsumi* is a derivative of a word meaning "imprudent." The fearful aspect in the term is not so much related to moral wrong as the potential of being discovered in a shameful act and losing face. This would put a person out of harmony with society and nature. Translators had to discuss whether this was the primary word they should use for sin.[35]

Linguists also face the intimidating task of discovering the overall structure of the language—how many vowels, how many consonants, regular and irregular verb forms, tenses, sentence structures, and much more.

When Kitty and Leslie Pride were working on the Chatino language of Mexico, at first it seemed as if only about thirty verbs were regular, leaving two hundred irregular verbs! They'd just about resigned themselves to rote memorization of the irregular verbs when Kitty noticed one verb with the prefix *ntya*. Mystified, she asked her language assistant about it. The assistant explained that this was the Chatino construction for passive verbs. To keep their words brief, they added *ntya* and dropped the middle of each verb. Gratefully, Pride learned that 170 Chatino verbs were neatly classified, regular verbs, leaving only thirty irregular ones.[36]

---

34 Beekman and Callow, *Translating the Word of God*, 123.
35 David Hesselgrave, *Communicating Christ Cross-culturally* (Grand Rapids: Zondervan, 1978), 268–69.
36 Pride, *Bread Is Not Enough*, 152–53.

The emphasis on verbs in some tongues requires that when nouns refer to events they must quite generally be back-transformed into verbal expressions. This can render Scripture in vividly simple phraseology. For example, the phrase "the beauty of holiness" from 2 Chronicles 20:21 becomes "being holy is beautiful."[37]

Some languages even mark the *function* of a message in rather explicit ways. For example, in Lisu, a language of southeast Asia, the sentence *Asa la-a ni* means "Asa is coming" and indicates the speaker is talking to himself. *Asa la-a lu* expresses the identical thing as information for others. In contrast, *Asa la-a na* has an imperative function—that is, the speaker expects some action or change of opinion when people hear it. *Asa la-a xu* reflects a complaint about Asa's coming, and sympathy is expected from hearers.[38]

Languages such as Huave and Aguacatec have what is called pronominal grammar. For example, if a linguist quoted Peter at Pentecost, "These men are not drunk, as you suppose" (Acts 2:15), he must be careful not to represent Peter as saying, "Though the others are not drunk, I certainly am."[39]

In a somewhat similar case, when a tribesman reads Paul's statement, "I can do everything through him who gives me strength" (Phil 4:13) in their language, Paul is saying he can do *anything*, but the unfortunate reader is excluded from such blessing.[40] And in the Zapotec language, when one reads Paul's challenge, "neither let us commit sexual immorality," the translator must be careful not to imply that Paul, too, had committed fornication or was in imminent danger of doing so.[41]

While working with the Dahomey of West Africa, a translator quoted John 8:12 where Jesus said, "I am the light of the world," They immediately thought Jesus had dubbed the *translator* the light of the world. "If Jesus says you are the light of the world," the Dahomey said enthusiastically, "we will gladly follow you. What is

---

[37] Eugene Nida, *Language Structure and Translation: Essays*, ed. Anwar Dil, Language Science and National Developmentn (Stanford: Stanford University Press, 1975), 81.
[38] Nida and Waard, *One Language to Another*, 31.
[39] Beekman and Callow, *Translating the Word of God*, 47.
[40] Ibid., 108.
[41] Ibid., 116.

it you want us to do?" In their language direct and indirect language must be specific. The verse had to read specifically, "*Jesus said* that he is the Light of the world."[42] Translators must constantly keep such rules of language in mind.

In the Mixe language of Mexico, when someone speaks of himself or herself in the third person it is because of shame over what one has done and is an attempt to hide it. So when Jesus says, "Foxes have holes . . . but the Son of Man has no place . . ." (Luke 9:58) or when John identifies himself only as "the disciple whom Jesus loved" (John 13:23; 19:26; 21:7,20), they are assumed to be doing so out of guilt or shame.[43]

Direct and indirect methods of speech vary from culture to culture. For example, the NIV translation renders Christ as saying to the man healed at Bethesda, "See, you are well again. Stop sinning or something worse may happen to you" (John 5:14). In the Chewa culture, this is an extremely rude portrayal of Christ. A good Chewa translation would read something like, "As you are now healthy like this, it would be good for you not to do wrong lest even worse troubles may arrive at your door."

Matthew 20:21 portrays Jesus as saying to the mother of James and John, "What is it you want?" The polite way of saying this in Chewa culture would be "Yes, mother. Can I help?"[44] Similarly, politeness for the Mangga Buang would dictate indirect language. Instead of "Your daughter is dead" (Mark 5:35; Luke 8:49), they'd say, "Your daughter's eyes are closed." And the Twi of Africa would be similarly indirect: "She has gone to her village."[45]

In the book of Ruth, to render literally several things Naomi told her daughters-in-law would be considered by the Tonga obnoxious language. For example, when she told them to return to their mothers' homes, she would be implying that they'd failed domestically and must get further training. And it should be made clear that she isn't

---

42 Ibid., 43.
43 Ibid., 114.
44 Ernst Wendland, *The Cultural Factor in Bible Translation* (New York, United Bible Societies, 1987), 150.
45 Mildred Larson, *Meaning-based Translation: A Guide to Cross-language Equivalence* (New York: University Press of America, 1984), 116.

mocking them when she says that if she married and had intercourse that night, would they wait to marry the sons that may result?[46]

In some languages, rhetorical questions are restricted almost entirely to ridicule.[47] In others, rhetorical questions are understood only as inquisitive questions. For example, when Jesus asked, "What shall we say the kingdom of God is like?"(Mark 4:30), native readers imagined that Jesus was asking out of ignorance.[48] Similarly, when the translator came to Paul's self-deprecating statement in 1 Corinthians 3:5, "Who then is Paul?" (KJV), the Trique language assistant looked puzzled. "Didn't Paul know who he was?" he asked. Realizing it must be translated differently if the Triques were to understand Paul's intent, the translator rendered Paul as saying, "Paul is not important," and the readers understood.[49]

Another challenge has to do with the contact use of language. In southern China, the Nushu language is spoken only by women, and in some regions, the erudite speak one form of a language and the lower classes use another. Which do translators select? Also, in some parts of the Arabic world, use of a colloquial form of language is appropriate only for comic strips and pornographic literature.[50]

When scholars set about the task of translating the Bible into vernacular Japanese during the 1950s, they hit a roadblock. For many Japanese, the highly literary style of the classical language seemed more appropriate for the message of sacred Scriptures. However, one verbal form in particular introduced an element of tentativeness into many factual statements of Scripture. Was it appropriate for a message based on faith in the unseen God to be expressed tentatively?[51]

In Haiti the common citizen speaks Haitian Creole, but French is used in higher education and government. It is possible to standardize a language like Haitian Creole, but it's a ticklish process.

---

46 Wendland, *The Cultural Factor*, 168.
47 D. Shaw, *Transculturation*, 215.
48 Beekman and Callow, *Translating the Word of God*, 245.
49 Hefley, *Searchlight on Bible Words*, 150.
50 Nida, *Language Structure and Translation*, 182.
51 Hesselgrave, *Communicating Christ Cross-culturally*, 48.

A premature attempt to use such a language for higher functions would be rejected as inappropriate or even ludicrous.[52]

Also, in certain languages, various terms, syntactic constructions, and rhetorical devices serve to mark varying kinds and levels of personal relationship. If speaking to friends, people use different words than if speaking to authorities. Sometimes there are even distinct differences between men's and women's speech. Which forms translators should use becomes a difficult and sometimes uncomfortable question.[53]

Scriptural repetition even implies varied things in different languages. For instance, the regular repetition of phrases and thoughts as in Hebrew poetry is regarded as rather insulting to some, as if the reader isn't intelligent enough to comprehend the thought the first time it is presented.[54]

For example, among the Hiligaynon of the Philippines, translating Christ's introductory words, "Truly, truly," does not underline the emphasis but lowers the emphasis to mean "perhaps." In their language, saying "truly" once would provide greatest emphasis.[55]

After linguists complete a translation, much work is still ahead. The spelling of names and concepts must be consistent. Key terms and phrases must be logged meticulously. The translator must make sure the words used are acceptable and appropriate to all who use that language or dialect. Then each book of the Bible must be compared with others for consistency and accuracy.[56]

It doesn't help for a translator to be almost accurate. For example, David and Kathleen Glasgow thought they had found the word for "whosoever" in the Burera language when they heard the word *an-nedi*. However, this word alone meant "strange ones." Obviously the promise of eternal life was not limited to strange people (at least, we hope not). The Glasgows had to add *marlaka* to *an-nedi* to form the word "anyone" or "whoever."

---

52 William Stewart, "Creole Languages in the Caribbean," in *Study of the Role of Foreign Languages in Asia, Africa, and Latin America*, ed. by Frank A. Rice (Washington DC: Center for Applied Linguistics, 1962), 49.
53 Nida and Waard, *One Language to Another*, 27–29.
54 Nida, *Language Structure and Translation*, 87.
55 Ibid., 25.
56 Shetler, *And the Word Came*, 145.

Some languages are characterized by sounds very foreign to those in the West—sounds such as nasalizations, clicks, and glottal fricatives (gutturals from the back of the throat).

In the Cakchiquel language of Guatemala, only a faint click distinguishes between the word for "Savior" and the word for "deceiver." So similar are the pronounciations that linguist John Beekman reported that it took his untrained ear about five years to distinguish clearly between them.[57]

Tonal factors also add to a language's complexity. In other words, expressions spelled exactly the same way can mean up to three or four different things, depending on the pitch or tone used. This makes it vital to have all accent marks accurate in written form.

Mazatec is a language in which tone or pitch is important. Just by changing the tone, a person can mean either "water" or "cactus." Another tone can mean either "his trousers" or "his leaf." Each syllable may be said in one of four basic pitches or sequence of pitches. The exact pitch varies depending on the gender of the speaker and even the mood of the speaker. Tone is so significant in Mazatec that sometimes people can communicate messages by simply whistling the lilt and cadence of the corresponding spoken phrase.[58]

In the Mixteco Indian dialect, each syllable has either a high, mid, or low tone, and particular words can exert an influence on other words, causing their pitch to change.[59] The same string of letters is used for "I am laughing" and "I am crying." The only difference, again, is a subtle tone. The word used for "I am laughing" ends in a high tone on the final syllable, while the word for "I am crying" has a low tone. A tribesman with laryngitis would have serious problems.[60]

There are cultures anthropologists would call "visual." They want, as much as possible, for communication to be both visible and tangible. Faith is illustrated often through drama, dance, painting, carving, and architecture. Some languages use music as a primary means of communication. This may grate against those with a

---

[57] Translation Treasures, *In Other Words*, April–June 1972.
[58] Pike, *Words Wanted*, 28–29.
[59] Pike, *Not Alone*, 45.
[60] Translation Treasures, *In Other Words*, April–June 1972, 15.

Western mindset where thought is more often abstract. We in the West are very verbal and like to discuss and debate our faith intellectually. Our church services may seem somewhat dry and monotonous to those from a visual culture. They integrate Scripture into visual display and focus on experiential expression and learning.[61]

Bruce Olson gives an account in which tribesmen of the Motilone in Colombia discussed the gospel through a song duel. Olson comments honestly that this chanted communication, sung back and forth by men swinging in hammocks tied to rafters, wasn't his favorite type of communication. But hours later the old chief climbed down and said, "God has spoken to us in song," and the whole house turned to Christ.[62]

Talk about tones and pitches—the Culina Indians of Peru also sing much of their language! The women sing to the men when they think the men should go hunting; then the men sing back to the women songs of the hunt. The men sing to the women as they return from a hunt, and the women respond with a song of welcome. And on it goes.

Since the Culinas' language is so musical, linguists Patsy Adams and Arlene Agnew have prepared many hymns and adapted them to the five-note or pentatonic scale which the Culinas follow. Interestingly, Culinas may sing each phrase of a song eight times or more before moving on to the next line. The repetition gives them time to assimilate the message and accustom their ears to any strange new names.

Having been spirit worshipers, the Culinas are often tempted to return to witchcraft and animism. One Culina hymn (based on 1 Pet 5:8,9) is sung when they're experiencing a severe testing:

> Now you all must, you must beware,
> And the eyes of all of you,
> You must keep them open;
> Because Satan just like a tiger is, he is
> He goes about, looking for you;

---

61 Wayan Mastra, cited in John Stott and Robert Coote, eds., *Gospel and Culture* (Pasadena: William Carey Library, 1979), 365–66.
62 Bruce Olson, *Bruchko* (Carol Stream, IL: Creation House, 1978), 152–53.

> He is seeking roundabout
> To finish you off, thus says God's Word.[63]

Try to imagine thousands of unique languages and dialects like Culina or Mazatec scattered among cultures in jungles, deserts, and cities throughout the earth. The goal of Christian translators is to render at least a portion of the Scriptures into every language on the planet. And they're completely convinced the task is doable by the power and grace of God.

---

63 Hefley, *Searchlight on Bible Words*, 166.

CHAPTER THREE

# Matching Scripture with Culture

Putting eternal truths into the speech of everyday life reflects exactly the style of the word of God. The New Testament books were not written in the high-flown Asian style of the schoolmasters of the first and second centuries AD. They were couched in the words of the common people who were seeking the truth about the living, risen Christ. For those who sought life, the dead forms of outmoded grammatical styles were useless. So today the missionary translator carries on that same tradition, giving people the words of God in the cultural language of the marketplace.[64] Though some idioms may seem strange to us, actually, biblical cultures and idioms are more similar to many other world cultures than they are to Western industrialized culture.[65]

When Christians fail to render the word of God in the cultural context of given native peoples, individuals often react the way a young Liberian did. As the Scriptures were presented to him in a "modern" form, they seemed to be saying, "God so loves Europeans that he accepts as Christian any African who turns his back on his

---

64 Eugene Nida, *God's Word in Man's Language* (New York: Harper & Row, 1952), 23.
65 D. Shaw, *Transculturation*, 48.

own customs and becomes converted to Western culture."[66] How can Bible linguists avoid communicating this?

The translator's personal background, historical period, cultural heritage, and ecological environment all intertwine to make it very difficult to translate the Bible in a way that fits the worldview of particular receptor cultures.[67] As long as the gospel doesn't fit into the context and meanings of a local culture, in the eyes of the people of that culture it will always be a "foreign religion."

Besides these hurdles, language can also be very weird. An expression in one language can mean something so different in another language that it throws us back on our heels. Who would ever guess that the Finnish slang, "He is sitting in his hotel," actually means "He is in prison"?[68]

When facing a passage of Scripture, the translator first attempts to match biblical words or phrases with literal terms in the receptor language. This is possible in many cases. However, when there is no matching term in the receptor language, a legitimate cultural substitute must be found in the idiom of the people. In this book we are making the terms "cultural substitute" and "functional equivalent" synonymous. For our purposes, a cultural substitute is a word or concept in the receptor language that is equivalent in function to a word or concept in the Bible.

Bible linguists are under a constant tension. The tension is between historical fidelity and dynamic fidelity. On the one hand, they can try to describe events, objects, or living things known only in the ancient world. This can result in gross misunderstanding of portions of the original message. On the other hand, they wish to avoid as often as possible the substitution of words or concepts known only in more recent historical periods. Their goal is to retain both historic and dynamic consistency, but occasionally there are cases in which they must make an agonizing choice which slightly favors one side or the other.[69]

---

[66] Charles Kraft, *Christianity in Culture* (Maryknoll, NY: Orbis Books, 1979), 289.
[67] Wendland, *The Cultural Factor*, 191.
[68] Larson, *Meaning-based Translation*, 116.
[69] Beekman and Callow, *Translating the Word of God*, 206.

Translating the Christian message into another culture is not without its danger and controversy. For example, in a Nigerian culture where a common proverb is "You cannot trust a man with one wife," should translators at least temporarily render one requirement of a deacon: "managing a *polygamous* household well"?[70] Christians may strongly disagree on an issue such as this; all the same, if a spiritual dialogue remains open between the believers who transmitted the message and the church that is now re-expressing its faith using fresh theology and practice, then it ought to be possible to avoid most of the pitfalls and to correct the errors to which both sides are still liable.

Many cultures rest upon a delicate balance of factors that keep the society relatively peaceful and on an even keel. For example, in a culture that is communitarian or very group oriented, one practice which tends to disrupt the balance is lack of respect for one's ancestors, and the other relates to how one views sorcery or witchcraft.[71] To these people the hierarchy of spiritual powers is important, as well as the need for mediation to preserve fellowship in the community. If missionaries disparage the worship of ancestors and deny the preeminence of sorcery, they must be able to show how Christ and the Christian faith are infinitely greater as functional equivalents than their former beliefs.[72] Throughout this book we will look at cultural substitutes that cover the gamut of Christian faith and practice; in this chapter we will begin with simpler, more concrete examples.

Bible translators disagree to some degree as to exactly when and how often functional equivalents should be used and when literal biblical words or concepts should be retained. For example, some believe that if the Bible speaks of Jacob using mandrakes, even if mandrakes are unknown in a culture, the translation should read something like: "Jacob used a plant with purplish flowers called a mandrake." If boats or anchors are unknown in a culture, the translator should render such a reference, "Our hope in Christ is steadfast,

---

70 D. Shaw, *Transculturation*, 68.
71 Daniel von Allmen, "The Birth of Theology: Contextualization as the Dynamic Element in the Formation of the New Testament," *International Review of Mission* 64, no. 253 (January 1975): 52.
72 Wendland, *The Cultural Factor*, 50–51.

like irons called anchors tied with ropes to a boat so the boat can go no farther" (Heb 6:19).[73] Or if, in a culture, a burial platform is utilized in mourning instead of sackcloth and ashes, the translator might render Matthew 11:21: "Just as you sit on the burial platform and wail in grief, so the foreigners of Tyre and Sidon would have put on sackcloth and ashes in grief for their sins."

Obviously the translation can become a bit ponderous when rendered in this manner, and carrying such a Bible around would require several wheelbarrows. It is understandable why some translators decide to resort to simple cultural substitutes, especially if a receptor culture is very isolated and extremely different from biblical cultures.[74]

It should never be imagined that translators decide on functional equivalents lightly. Bible translation is taken very seriously, and they try to look at all the angles before substituting another word or phrase for one in the biblical text. J. B. Phillips calls this process *reflective digestion.*[75]

A translator may try many substitutes before an appropriate one is found. For example, in Revelation 18:19 people are portrayed as throwing dust on their heads as a sign of mourning when the city of Babylon is destroyed. In seeking a functional equivalent for throwing dust, a linguist learned of the bereavement custom of throwing sand backwards over the shoulder. Further inquiry, however, revealed that the practice was only used at the death of a loved one, so it was dropped from consideration.[76]

In another culture, translators debated whether to substitute the familiar skin disease, *pinto*, for the disease of leprosy. Native speakers had never heard of leprosy, but *pinto* was similar to it in various ways. However, to use *pinto* implied that biblical writers recognized the illness, and this was not historically accurate.

One solution is to make certain cultural substitutes temporary. In other words, as the initial books of the Bible are translated, linguists

---

73 Larson, *Meaning-based Translation*, 170–71.
74 Ibid., 172.
75 J. B. Phillips, *The New Testament in Modern English* (New York: Macmillan, 1958), x.
76 Beekman and Callow, *Translating the Word of God*, 205.

may use cultural substitutes liberally. However, as native speakers come to better understand the ancient biblical cultures, some of the cultural substitutes are replaced with literal terms.[77]

For example, when James 3:12 was originally translated into Aguaruna, the linguist tried describing literal figs, olives, and vines. However, when read, it resulted in such distracting debates about what the fruits were like that the three were replaced with two native fruits and the native palm tree. The translator planned to return to the original terms when readers became more familiar with such biblico-cultural facts.[78]

Animals are often used as illustrations in the Scriptures. In the English-speaking world, we associate certain traits with particular animals and sometimes use the name of the animal to refer to the trait. For example, foxes are considered sly and crafty, donkeys as stupid and stubborn, goats as mean and obstinate, pigs as filthy and greedy. However, in many other cultures the animals do not symbolize these same traits.

In the Bible, some animals are used to symbolize contrasting qualities. For example, in places, snakes are used to symbolize wisdom or shrewdness and in other places, craftiness and evil.

In Matthew 10, Jesus challenged his followers to be "wise as serpents." This would not make sense to the Tonga or Chewa reader. These tribespeople hate snakes; the only emotions they conjure are fear, distrust, and pain. The proposal to substitute *kalulu* (hare) was not much better because of connotations associated with the amoral trickster in tribal folklore.[79]

John the Baptist's reproachful nickname for the godless crowds was "brood of vipers" (Matt 3:7; Luke 3:7). However, among the Balinese people the viper is regarded as a snake of paradise. John the Baptist would be actually giving the people a nice compliment. For the Balinese, it would be better to use perhaps a more generic term like "vermin."[80]

---

77 Ibid., 209.
78 Ibid., 211.
79 Wendland, *The Cultural Factor*, 117.
80 Nida and Reyburn, *Meaning across Cultures*, 54.

Joe Grimes translated the Bible into the Huichol language of west central Mexico. We can peer briefly into Joe's mind as he attempted to translate the term "brood of vipers."

First of all, there are no vipers in the Western hemisphere. Grimes realized he could simply try to describe literally for the Indians what John was expressing: "You people are as dangerous and untrustworthy as your ancestors were." But Grimes felt that the description weakened John's expression, killed his metaphor, and slowed down the rhythm of the passage.

Joe considered using the phrase "brood of rattlesnakes," but in Huichol, when "a brood" doesn't refer to blood descendants, it is a metaphor for people who adhere to someone or consider the person a role model. Those who support a politician, for example, would be that politician's brood.

Third observation: traditional Huichol folktales laud the rattlesnake as the epitome of wisdom. He is sent beneficently by Tavexicua, the sun god, to warn people. Thus, to the Huichols, "brood of rattlesnakes" would communicate something like "you people have certainly chosen wise role models for yourselves." Since we believe John was actually expressing "you people perpetuate the deadly ideas of your ungodly tradition," Grimes knew he had more work to do.

Next, Grimes searched for a substitute for "brood." When describing objects or people who are alike, the Huichols often refer to them as siblings. For example, when Grimes arrived among the Huichols in a Volkswagen Beetle, they called it "the Armadillo." When they learned that his Volkswagen Camper, which arrived a few years later, was made by the same factory, they called it "Armadillo's Brother." Grimes realized he could substitute "brothers of" for "brood."

Grimes continued to look for a substitute for viper or rattlesnake. He considered the coral snake, but recognized that the Huichols knew the snake as very shy and retiring. This did not at all imply the dangerous aggressiveness John seemed to have in mind.

Then Grimes thought of the *Centruoides suffuses*, a medium-sized, straw-colored scorpion whose sting kills children and occasionally adults. The scorpion is fast-moving and unpredictable, lives in and around Huichol houses, falls down out of thatched roofs at night and generally stings whatever or whoever it lights upon.

Having a scorpion as one's role model would indeed be an insult, as John's statement was. "Brothers to scorpions" was a lively metaphor which communicated instantly and accurately to readers both the feeling of malignant evil and the risk of being around these people.[81]

Similarly, in the Cheyenne language John the Baptist's "brood of vipers" has no meaning and carries no idea of slippery danger. To the Cheyenne, it is *coyotes* that are sly and deceptive, so translators used coyotes instead of vipers. Tribespeople even call each other coyotes in condemnation of deceit and destructiveness.[82]

In Luke 13:32 Jesus addresses Herod as a fox and, as in English, he seems to have been alluding to his tricky, slippery nature. But the fox happens to symbolize a contrasting variety of figures in various cultures. To the Maxakali of Brazil a fox is a redhead, to the Zapotes of Villa Alta a fox is someone who cries a lot, for the Otomi of Mexico it is a chicken thief, for the Cuicatecs of Teutilo it alludes to a good hunter, to the Pame it indicates one who cruelly kills domesticated animals, and in some parts of Central America it refers to a homosexual.[83]

In the Alekano tribe, where foxes are unknown, it is more accurate to render the quote, "Go tell that man with the soul of a dog ..."[84] The Sochiapan Chinantec Indians know of nothing that more typifies a tricky, deceitful liar than an opossum. To call a person an opossum is a great insult. David Foris' language assistants thought it very appropriate to word Paul's powerful rebuke of Elymas the sorcerer, "You opossum son of the devil ..." (Acts 13:10). This one word says more to these Indians than would a long string of adjectives.[85]

Wild dogs are substituted for wolves in Matthew 7:15 because Alekanos have never heard of wolves. The Amahuaca Indians also have no concept of wolves, but since tigers have been known to attack and kill domestic animals in villages, in John 10:12 where Jesus

---

81 Joe Grimes, email message to author, December 1, 2001.
82 Wayne Leman, email message to author, November 29, 2001.
83 Marvin Mayers, *Christianity Confronts Culture: A Strategy for Cross-cultural Evangelism* (Grand Rapids: Zondervan, 1974), 61.
84 Beekman and Callow, *Translating the Word of God*, 138–39.
85 David Foris, email message to author, November 28, 2001.

speaks of wolves killing sheep, tigers are substituted for wolves.[86] And because Chewas of East Africa don't associate wild donkeys with nomadic roaming, as when the angel describes Ishmael as a "wild donkey of a man" (Gen 16:12), it is much clearer to Chewas rendered: "He shall become a wildcat."[87]

The Inupiat Eskimos have no words for animals such as the horse, pig, or camel. Translators had to use the closest equivalents. Horse became "like a big caribou." Swine became "queer caribous," and camel became a "humpbacked carrier." The equivalents must enable people to get the point which the biblical author intended. For example, hopefully the Eskimos got the point in Mark 10:35: "It is easier for a 'humpbacked carrier' to go through the eye of a needle than for a rich man to enter into the kingdom of God."[88]

Interpreting the same verse for the Iquito Indians, Bob Eastman wasn't sure how the Iquitos described the eye of a needle. When he threaded a needle in front of his Indian helper, the man said, "You are putting the string through the needle's ear." So for the Iquitos the verse read: "It is harder for a camel to enter a needle's ear than for a rich man to enter God's country."[89]

Of course, functional equivalents extend far beyond the animal kingdom. Some relate to what is appropriate between individuals. For example, portions of the Song of Solomon seem rather vulgar in the Tonga culture of Zambia. In 1:2 the maiden longs for kisses. To the Tongas, kissing is suitable only between a mother and her baby. They would view a girl this brazen to surely be a prostitute. Later the writer compares his lover's eyes to those of a dove, but the Tonga dove has red eyes, and if a woman has red eyes it's a sign of either drunkenness or witching. The teeth are described as shorn ewes, supposedly emphasizing their whiteness. A Tonga woman would rather have her teeth compared to those of a cow, and besides that, a woman *missing* her four front teeth is considered more attractive than one with all her teeth. The author of the song writes of being ravished by his lover's gaze, but a young Tonga woman must be coy.

---

86 Hefley, *Searchlight on Bible Words*, 13.
87 Wendland, *The Cultural Factor*, 130.
88 Hefley, *Searchlight on Bible Words*, 14.
89 Ibid., 175.

She should never look at a Tonga male directly, but only roll her eyes while glancing away, showing the male the white of the eye. In 4:15 the lover describes the bride as a well of fresh water and a flowing spring. This would only suggest to a Tonga that the young woman is ill with diarrhea or perhaps an infection of the urogenital tract.[90]

Translators must also be aware of aspects of village life. When translators working among the Muyuws of New Guinea reached 1 Corinthians 3:6: "I planted the seed, Apollos watered it, but God made it grow," they realized that rainfall was such that the natives didn't need to water their gardens. So they rendered the verse: "I planted the seed, Apollos put in the stakes [up which the plants climb] and God made it grow."[91]

In Acts 12:13, after Peter was miraculously released from prison, he went and knocked on the door at the home of John Mark's mother. Among some peoples of Southeast Asia, Peter's knocking on the door might mean he was feeling romantic. To them "knocking on doors" is considered a signal from a lover who wants a rendezvous with a girlfriend.[92]

The Bora Indians of Peru do not have doors and never knock on entryways to announce their arrival. So when translating the story about Peter coming to John Mark's home, the translators considered writing, "Peter hammered on the entrance," but instead they decided to use an approach the Boras would definitely understand. They just wrote, "He [Peter] called, 'Are you there?'"[93]

The Amahuaca people also live in crude huts without doors, so a translator translated John 10:9: "I am the entrance," instead of "I am the door" (KJV).[94]

Similarly, another group that does not have doors is the Zanaki people of Zimbabwe. Early preachers to the Zanaki translated Revelation 3:20: "Behold I stand at the door and knock. If anyone hears my voice and opens the door, I will come in . . ." Obviously this was not appropriate.

---

90 Wendland, *The Cultural Factor*, 3–4.
91 Larson, *Meaning-based Translation*, 172.
92 Nida and Reyburn, *Meaning across Cultures*.
93 Hefley, *Searchlight on Bible Words*, 140.
94 Ibid., 15.

To enter the home of an acquaintance in a Zanaki village, one calls out loudly at the doorway. The only people who knock on the doorpost are thieves who do not want to be identified. If the thieves hear stirring inside, they immediately sneak away. Thus preachers were actually implying that Jesus was no more than a thief.

An appropriate translation of Revelation 3:20 in Zanaki might be: "Behold I stand at the door and call out. If anyone hears my voice and invites me inside, I will enter and eat with him and he with me."[95]

In various languages, wineskins in Mark 2:22 become "old gourds." Figs and grapes in Luke 6:44 become "bananas and pandanus." And in Job 39:15, breaking an egg becomes "killing an egg."[96]

The equivalent word for bread in some cultures would be cake, an item eaten only as an occasional treat. But when Jesus referred to himself as the Bread of Life, he was certainly not implying his availability to meet human spiritual need only on an occasional basis.[97] In still another culture, nothing like bread is made or eaten; the baker in the story of God's providential care of Joseph becomes "one who makes foreign tortillas."

Among a people where there are no sandals, Matthew 3:11 reads, "I am not worthy to carry his shoulder bag." And in a culture that has no concept of the wheel and axle, a chariot becomes "an instrument of carrying one, with two round feet which mules pull."[98]

Among the Bamileke people, the idiom in Psalm 30:11, "you removed my sackcloth" could be vividly rendered, "you have taken the bag of mourning from my hand," since in Bamileke society mourners carry a *raffia* bag over the arm. And Paul's warning that the spiritual soldier doesn't get involved in "civilian affairs" (2 Tim 2:4) could be pictured perfectly for Balinese in the clause, "the Christian warrior doesn't carry a market bag."[99]

---

95 Michael Frost, "Translating the Gospel," Centre for Evangelism and Global Mission, http://www.cegm.org (accessed September 26, 2001), 2.
96 Larson, *Meaning-based Translation*, 144.
97 David Foris, email message to author, November 28, 2001.
98 Hefley, *Searchlight on Bible Words*, 172.
99 Nida and Reyburn, *Meaning across Cultures*, 55–56.

In addition to the need for word or phrase substitutions, idioms or figures of speech differ widely from one culture to another. For example, in the Chewa language the Hebrew idiom for the oath, "May the Lord do so to me and more . . ." is rendered: "May lightning [from God] tear me if . . ."[100]

Among the Tsongas, to "lack a head" is to be stupid, to "have a long heart" is to be patient, to "crush a bug" is to use foul language (for them, crushing a bug usually releases a stink), to "bite the ear" is to eat the firstfruits of the season, and to "tie the tongue" is to be silent (similar to the English expression "tongue-tied").[101]

Luke 18:13 speaks of a publican beating his breast in humble contrition. In contrast, the Cuicatecos beat their chests to show machismo, Otomi Indians do it to reflect rage, West Africans do it to show pride of accomplishment (similar to the English expression "pat oneself on the back"), and the Batswana people of South Africa do so to reflect self-assurance and aggressiveness.[102]

Conversely, to the Batswanas a gesture of contrition would be to "take hold of the beard." Contrition or humble regret in another African language is expressed by the phrase "clubbing one's own head."[103] Speaking of regret, in the Middle East sitting in sackcloth and ashes reflected penitence or mourning, but among the Cuiatecos a different expression would have to be used because a lazy bum sitting by the fire is spoken of as "sitting in ashes."

J. I. Packer's searching questions on cross-cultural communication can easily be applied to the hundreds of functional equivalence issues that arise.

Is a Bible translation calculated to divert attention away from the merely earthly to God and his truth? Does it make the gospel sound like a human idea, a preacher's plaything . . . ? Does it smack of human cleverness and showmanship, or does it embody rather the straightforward, unaffected simplicity . . . of one who desires to blot himself out, fearing nothing so much as that people should admire and applaud him when they ought to be humbling themselves before

---

100 Wendland, *The Cultural Factor*, 170.
101 Nida and Waard, *One Language to Another*, 153.
102 Beekman and Callow, *Translating the Word of God*, 122.
103 Nida and Waard, *One Language to Another*, 74.

the mighty Lord whom he represents?[104] These are the hard questions translators must ask as they begin work with a new language.

---

104 J. I. Packer, *Evangelism and the Sovereignty of God* (Chicago: InterVarsity, 1961), 87.

CHAPTER FOUR

# The Search for God in Every Culture

One vital issue with which translators struggle is how to identify the God of the Bible in a new culture. Some believe that the Hebrew four letters YHWH (spelled Yahweh in English) constitute the proper name for the biblical God. Ancient Jewish people considered this name so holy that it was not to be uttered except in the most sublime occasions. Yet the infinite God is so complex that, even in the Bible, there are numerous names to represent him: Adonai, Elohim, El Elyon, Jehovah Jireh, El Shaddai, Immanuel, Son of God, and Savior comprise only a few. Bible translators must start out with one identifying name.

There are three general choices:

(1) Discover a god in the existing culture, the description of whom has characteristics sufficiently close to those which characterize the biblical God. This may assume that the people were innately worshiping the Creator God without yet knowing the gospel or the biblical message.

(2) Select a new descriptive title never before used in the language to be translated, which will be quite meaningless until nationals learn to know the biblical God.

(3) Choose a combination of words or parts of words borrowed from the native language, which carry meaning corresponding to biblical deity.

There appear to be many more examples of the first strategy listed above than the second or third so we will limit our examples primarily to the idea of selecting an already existing name for God. Coining an entirely new word for God is rarely tried, and borrowing words or combinations of such has not often proved successful.

Eugene Nida states that some translators, in employing a borrowed term for "God," have assumed that the native people will automatically come to understand the meaning another culture has invested in the title, but in most cases the native immediately tries to equate this meaningless word for God with his own belief system. For example, the Aztecs equated Dios with the sun, the Virgin Mary with the moon, and Jesus as the offspring of the two.[105]

Some criticize translators for selecting the name of a current god in a culture as synonymous with the God of the Bible. However, if this god is known as the supreme creator of the universe and already has been attributed qualities similar to the true God of the Bible, some translators see no inherent problem in using that term. David Livingstone testified that "there is no necessity for beginning to tell even the most degraded of these people of the existence of a God, or of a future state, the facts being universally admitted."[106]

Abraham had no problem tithing to Melchizedek (Cf. Gen 14:18–20), a king of righteousness having no beginning or end. In Athens, the Apostle Paul didn't hesitate to identify the Greeks' elusive "Unknown God" as the true God of the Bible. And some centuries later, such missionaries as Matthew Ricci used ancient names for

---

[105] Nida, *Bible Translating*, 205.
[106] David Livingstone, *Missionary Travels and Researches in Central Africa* (London: John Murray, 1857), 158.

God such as the Chinese reference *Shang-Ti T'ien* (Sovereign Lord of Heaven).[107]

However, translators must be very careful to discern whether a revered god of a culture is really synonymous with the biblical God or his Son. Obviously the supposed Hindu "tenth incarnation of Vishnu" cannot be synonymous with Christ, nor can the Buddhists' fifth manifestation of Buddha, *Phra-Ariya-Metrai*, be identified as the Son of God. God incarnate cannot be a mere "fifth manifestation" of anyone.[108]

The Bontoc people of the Philippines told stories of a god named *Lomawig*. The people described how *Lomawig* had performed miracles and even descended from heaven. But it was only when translator Lawrence Reid questioned further that he became convinced he could not use this name for God. The Bontocs did not worship *Lomawig* nor admit that he had or deserved any influence over their affairs. Though Reid realized it was far from ideal, in the end he decided to use the term *Dios* for God since it was already a widespread Philippine term introduced by the Spanish.[109]

Many in the Mazatec tribe of Mexico worshiped the sun god. When Mazatecs first heard about Jesus, they immediately assumed that he was synonymous with the sun god. It was obvious to translator Eunice Pike that this was not appropriate. Even after reading Scripture, some Mazatecs continued to argue that the sun was God because they believe that without the sun god, there would be no crops and no life, but Pike stood firmly against this idea.[110]

Early in Catholic mission work among the Mayan people in what is now Mexico, Dominican Tomas de la Torre insisted that the designation *Cabahuil* or *Chi*, the chief Mayan god, should be made synonymous with the true God of the Bible instead of using the Spanish word *Dios*. He believed the word *Dios* carried absolutely no meaning for the Indians, while *Chi* was considered the Supreme God over all.

---

107 Ruth Tucker, *From Jerusalem to Irian Jaya: A Biographical History of Christian Missions* (Grand Rapids: Zondervan, 1983), 64.
108 Richardson, *Eternity in Their Hearts*, 56.
109 Hefley, *Searchlight on Bible Words*, 128–29.
110 Pike, *An Uttermost Part*, 20, 144.

The title for Jesus became *El Gran Chiman* (the Supreme Shaman-priest). In the Mayan culture, the term "shaman-priest" means the "profession of the holy." He is a leader and mediator chosen by God to enter the presence of spirits without suffering harm. This corresponds to Christ, who mediates constantly on behalf of the believer and who alone is able to protect the believer from evil spirits and from God's wrath.

Though the word *Chi* may have communicated more to the Mayans than did *Dios*, other flaws in the mission work resulted in spiritual confusion, even chaos. Many priests did not learn the Mayan language, few Scriptures were translated into Mayan, and some insisted that various Latin terms be retained instead of searching for functional equivalents. Mayans learned the sacraments and ceremonies but did not understand salvation and other crucial doctrines of Scripture. Bishop Ruiz of Chiapas admits that the people were more sacramentalized than evangelized.

This resulted in a faith that was simply integrated into their pagan rituals, yielding what some call Christo-paganism—a synthesis that is still pagan at its roots.[111] Christo-paganism is a serious problem that arises if translators aren't careful about word and concept choice and don't combine translation with instruction. The target people begin conveniently mixing pagan beliefs with biblical ones.

Thus some early Catholic missionaries administered sacraments and ceremonies but mixed bits of Mayan language with Latin and taught little Scripture in the vernacular. Mayans inevitably tried to piece together extremely sketchy ideas of the gospel, which they, in turn, attempted to reconcile with their superstitions. The following direct excerpts of common native beliefs illustrate the confusion and the pagan influence:

> Before, the earth was flat. Father Jose and Mother Maria Santissima were the first Indians. [Jose] made the earth, then came Maria, his wife, and then Jose made men. It was always night so Jose made a great machine called the Sun so he could see. Then Jesus Christo, the first son of Jose and Maria, was born.

---

111 Coke, *Translation among the Maya*, 97.

*The Search for God in Every Culture*

While Maria was pregnant, the Devil came to Jose and told him Maria had many lovers, but Jose did not believe it. Jesus Christo grew to full size in four days. When Christo made the mountains, the people of the Devil were angry and said, "We are not accustomed to these. It is better that we kill him." They looked for him for twenty days. They asked the turkeys and chickens . . . if Jesus had passed by. The animals were gossips and told the Jews where to look. Only the mules and horses were not gossips. For this, people do not kill them today, but they do sacrifice chickens and turkeys and especially cows.

Jesus ran from the Jews for more than forty days. One day the pursuers were close and Jesus found a dead horse. He hid in the stomach of the horse and the Jews could not find him. Then they finally caught Jesus and made him carry a large cross. The next day they crucified him. He suffered but was not dead; then a blind man came along and the Jews handed him a knife and said to stab. He didn't know what he was doing when he stabbed Jesus in the breast and ended his suffering.

Then they placed Jesus' body at the edge of the pueblo. A burro came and breathed over the body of Jesus and made the scars disappear. That same night Jesus went to heaven and has never returned. When the enemies returned, they couldn't find him and they were afraid. They hid behind trees in fear but a great storm broke and each flash of lightning killed one. Now only those who live beneath the ground where Jesus placed them are alive.[112]

In the centuries since this time, missionaries have corrected misconceptions by emphasizing the truth of Scripture, practical benefits of salvation through Christ, harmony in the community, forgiveness

---

[112] Mary Shaw, ed., *According to Our Ancestors* (Guatemala: Instituto Linguistico de Verano, 1971), 51–52.

of sin, and especially freedom from the vices common to Christo-paganism.[113]

Among the Fiji islanders, when a missionary spoke of God as *Ndina*, he assumed natives would realize that other gods were non-existent. However, the natives believed that, though *Ndina* was the most effective, reliable god, other gods may still be effective at times.[114]

The Mazatec Indians also developed some strange ideas about God which had to be corrected. Once when they saw a picture of some monkeys, someone said, "Look! Look at the men that became animals." When asked to explain, the Mazatecs related a story told by their elders that long, long ago there was a group of men who refused to say the catechism. So God made them into monkeys with tails, and they've been animals ever since.[115]

In another case, an African chief told linguist Charles Kraft this myth:

> Once God and his son lived close to us. They walked, talked, ate, and slept among us. All was well then. There was no thievery or fighting or running off with another man's wife like there is now. But one day God's son ate in the home of a careless woman. She had not cleaned her dishes properly. God's son ate from a dirty dish, got sick, and died. This, of course, made God very angry. He left in a huff and hasn't been heard from since.[116]

Then the chief asked, "White man, can you tell us how to get back into contact with this God?"[117]

The first tendency of some might be to rebuke the chief, point out how wrong the story was, and immediately relate the detailed account of Genesis. However, the wiser approach may be to refrain from contradicting or rebuking the chief and, instead, focus on the

---

113 Coke, *Translation among the Maya*, 236.
114 Edward Evans-Pritchard, *Theories of Primitive Religion* (London: Oxford University Press, 1965), 7–8.
115 Pike, *An Uttermost Part*, 92.
116 Kraft, *Christianity in Culture*, 153.
117 Ibid.

truths in the story: the existence of God and his Son, the alienation between people and God, and the resultant disintegration of human relationships. Then the door would be open to explain the salvation God offers and the necessity of a faith response to Christ as the means of restoring a peaceful relationship with God and then with fellow humans. Later, as the native people learn more from the Bible, they will realize the full truth.

As is evident, if missionaries and translators are not vigilant, it is easy for false beliefs about God to develop among a people and for these heresies to spread and become a movement. In his book, *Solomon Islands Christianity*, A. R. Tippett describes one such situation.

Silas Eto, a rather offbeat islander, founded a church offshoot which eventually split from traditional church groups. In fact, in the end Eto assumed the title *Holy Mama* (Holy Father) and took his place among the members of the Trinity. When Eto began as a church leader, his beliefs seemed quite orthodox. Then he attached himself to an eccentric, feisty mission sister who apparently modeled the independent arrogance that Eto eventually began to ape.[118]

Eto met Mormons, Jehovah's Witnesses, even Oral Roberts, and began trying to integrate tenets of each into his teachings. He bought into spiritual phenomena from the book *Battle for the Mind*, he experienced alleged visions, and he also came to idolize John Wesley and his "enthusiasms."

These influences and others resulted in a stick-tapping, flag-waving style of worship typified by "warmed heart" experiences (Wesley terminology), portrayed by members climbing church walls, flinging themselves to the floor, drumming with sticks, or passing into states of ecstasy.[119]

Especially in some of the hymns, Eto began to be substituted for Christ, and the teachings became increasingly Eto-centric; that is, the Holy Spirit was bearing witness to Silas Eto, not to Christ. If questioned on this matter, Etoists would reply that the work of Christ

---

[118] Alan Tippett, *Solomon Islands Christianity* (London: Lutterworth, 1967), 220, 222, 257.
[119] Ibid., 223.

was finished, and *Holy Mama's* had now begun.[120] Eto's meetings became increasingly similar to the Solomon Island ghost cult, thus classifying Etoism as a Christo-pagan religious syncretism.[121]

Finally, to prevent adherents from being exposed to differing beliefs, Eto closed the doors of their churches to all but loyal followers, thus making it a secret cult. To further suppress the truth, he declared the Bible to be like a dictionary, to be used only for occasional reference but never to be read through. He also claimed what American soldiers had told him—that the Bible was written by very fallible men and should only be interpreted by the *Holy Mama*.[122]

Despite such distortions of the identity of God, there have been many cases in which missionaries find that the name of a supreme, creator God is already known among a people who know nothing of the Bible. When contemporary missionary Efrain Alphonse sought the name of God among the Valiente Indians of Panama, it seemed a great mystery. Finally he was taken to an old medicine woman in the tropical forest. Lapsing into a trancelike state, the woman exclaimed, "These men are talking about *Ngobo*, the God of heaven and earth. Listen to them."[123]

When a missionary asked the Xhosa people, "What do you say about the creation of all things?" they replied, "We call him who made all things *uTikxo*. When asked, "Where is he?" the Xhosa said, "*Usezulwini*: he is in heaven." The missionary said that this was the God he wished to talk to them about.[124]

The Pawnee Indian tribe of North America had an intelligent appreciation of the God of heaven, whom they worshiped without any physical representation. In fact, Roman Catholic priests who visited their villages for the first time were amazed at their knowledge of the nature of God. The Indians even rejected crucifixes and figurines as being unsatisfactory representations of "holy ones." The Yakima tribe called the Creator God the Greatest Great and Highest High. In fact, a portion of an ancient Yakima prayer reads:

---

120 Ibid., 227.
121 Ibid., 256.
122 Ibid., 253, 263–64.
123 Nida, *God's Word*, 120.
124 Edwin Smith, *African Ideas of God* (London: Edinburgh House, 1950), 101.

> Oh You Greatest Great and Highest High,
> When you pass by this way stop and pity us,
> Not because we are worthy for we are most unworthy
> Not because we are good because our hearts are bad
> But because you made us and because we need you,
> And lead us to your everlasting life.[125]

The Ila of Zambia call God *Shikakunamo* (the Besetting One). In a Zambian myth a woman searches desperately for God, though countrymen keep telling her, "The Besetting One sits on the back of every one of us, and we cannot shake him off!" The idea seems to be that, though humans may search for God in many futile ways, just as Paul declared, "Indeed, he is close to each one of us" (Acts 17:27, Moffatt).

Many languages and dialects contain names for a number of gods, some originating in folk stories, mythologies, or standing religious beliefs. But when Wayne and Betty Snell were translating the Machiguenga language, they learned of a word for a supreme god.

"God," said a tribesman, "is the 'One who Blows.' He makes the trees and all good animals like the wild pig and tapir. The devil does all bad things—snakes, jaguar, wild bamboo . . . But God, the Blowing One, lives on a big mountain near a stream. No one can ever talk to him." The Snells decided that "the Blowing One" was a worthy word to use for the Creator God. They believed that as they educated the tribe regarding the true character of the biblical God, misconceptions such as his aloofness would drop away.

The Shona people of Africa allude to God's immutable omnipotence by calling him "the One who can turn things upside down." The Karanga speak of God as "the Great Pool, contemporary of everything" which, according to theologian John Mbiti, is suggested by the Zambezi River and its tributaries which annually flood the Karanga's region.[126]

In another case among the Kaka and Bulu tribes of Cameroon, the term *Ndjambie* was selected for the biblical God. What some may find disturbing is that the name originally referred to an

---

125 Fraser, *No Dark Valley*, 44, 139.
126 John Mbiti, *Concepts of God in Africa* (New York: Praeger, 1970), 5, 13.

impersonal, mythical cosmic spider. However, the Christians have infused completely new meaning into the word by investing it with denotations and connotations of the personal, infinite, Creator God of the Scriptures.[127]

When Rachel Saint was translating Scripture into the Waorani language, she found that their name for the Creator God was *Waengongi*, also the name for a species of fish. While the name did not inherently carry biblical attributes, it did not connote antibiblical concepts of God either. She decided to use it as the name of the God of Scripture. After studying the Bible, Christian Aucas now know *Waengongi* as the God of the Bible: infinite, eternal, always doing well, responding justly, showing anger regarding sin, loving, and saving, etc.

Some might say that since the word doubles as a fish it should have been disqualified, but almost every Auca proper name is equivalent to the name of some animal, plant, or bird. Saint found that the Aucas never equate the name of the person with the name of the natural object it may also represent.

In other words, if an Auca tribesman's name is *Komi*, and someone asks what the word means, they will reply, "Nothing. That is simply his name." It is only when an Auca picks up some string that they will call it *komi*. However, Aucas came to so revere *Waengongi*, the Creator God, that they eventually changed the name of the fish to *amo*.[128]

When Methodist missionaries first began work among the Zulu, they resisted using *uNkulunkulu*, the Zulu term for God. They coined the unwieldy term *uJehova*. Then an Anglican bishop among the Zulu tried to introduce the term *uDio*. Neither term, however, was accepted by the Zulu people. Finally, to the rejoicing of the nationals, the Zulu word for God was adopted.[129]

The Chinese call the Lord of heaven *Shang Ti*, and the Koreans call him *Hananim*, the Great One. With the centuries, the Chinese

---

[127] William Reyburn, "The Transformation of God and the Conversion of Man," *Practical Anthropology* 4 (1957): 185–94.

[128] Hefley, *Searchlight on Bible Words*, 133–34.

[129] Lamin Sanneh, *Translating the Message: The Missionary Impact on Culture* (Maryknoll, NY: Orbis Books, 1989), 171.

lost sight of *Shang Ti*'s merciful side and eventually ruled that only the emperor was great enough to stand in his awesome presence. Other gods filled the vacuum as the people searched for spiritual fulfillment. When missionaries went to China, there was argument about whether to use *Shang Ti* as the name for God. The disagreement became bitter, many thinking they must invent a new name for a new belief.

Conversely, the Protestant missionaries who arrived in Korea enthusiastically recognized *Hananim* as the biblical God. Koreans listened to them by the thousands, spellbound that these missionaries knew more about the true God than even their own king. The gospel spread in Korea in a way it never did in China.[130] The two largest Protestant churches in the world now exist in South Korea.

As far back as the 1920s a Wilhelm Schmidt set out to compile every alias of the Almighty that researchers had discovered. It took six volumes to compile them all, and over a thousand more examples have surfaced since then. The upshot of it all indicates that approximately 90 percent of all folk religions acknowledge the existence of one Supreme God.[131]

Even more powerful is evidence that the biblical God has actually prepared people groups throughout history to be interested, even longing, to know the Creator God. In his outstanding book *Eternity in Their Hearts*, Don Richardson describes many well-documented cases of this. Richardson bases the book on Solomon's statement in Ecclesiastes that God "set eternity in the hearts of men" (Eccl 3:11); that is, he has placed an innate longing for the Creator God within the souls of humans.

During the period when the Inca empire was at its height, King Pachacuti came to the conclusion that the Creator God they called *Viracocha* deserved recognition and worship much more than *Inti*, the sun god. He reaffirmed the omnipotent *Viracocha* as ancient, remote, supreme, and uncreated, manifesting himself as a trinity when he wishes; a God who ordains the times of humans and

---

130 Richardson, *Eternity in Their Hearts*, 68–69.
131 Ibid., 44.

nourishes them, and has pity on human wretchedness, warming them through his created son, *Punchao*, the sun disk.

Given that he had no access to the word of God, Pachacuti came surprisingly close to the truth. The king's major mistake was limiting worship of the Creator God only to the ruling caste, believing it to be too subtle and sublime for ordinary citizens. Thus, when the ruling class fell to the Spaniards, belief in *Viracocha* died out. Christian missionaries weren't present to translate the gospel into the Inca language. There was a vague prophecy that one day *Viracocha* would bring them blessing from the west by sea, but Pizarro and others appeared first, wreaking destruction.

During the nineteenth century, 2.5 million Santal people lived north of Calcutta, India. When a missionary named Lars Skrefsrud appeared among the Santal and explained the gospel, he heard them muttering that perhaps *Thakur Jiu* had not forgotten them after all. When he inquired, Skrefsrud learned that *Thakur* meant "genuine" and *Jiu* meant "god."

A village elder told the missionary the story of *Thakur Jiu*. *Jiu* had created the first man and woman far to the west of India. A being named *Lita* tempted them to make rice beer. They poured part of the beer on the ground as a sacrifice to Satan and became drunk on the rest. When they awoke, they knew they were naked and felt ashamed.

The children of this couple eventually migrated to a region where they became even more corrupted. When humans wouldn't listen to *Thakur Jiu*'s entreaties to return to him, he hid a holy pair on Mount Harata, and destroyed the rest of mankind with a flood.

During a later migration, the descendants of the holy pair became faint and frantic when they reached what seemed an insurmountable mountain chain. In their desperation, they forsook *Thakur Jiu* and called on the "mountain gods" for passage. When they found a way through the mountains, they attributed their survival to these gods and began the practice of spirit appeasement.

Skrefsrud realized how close the Santal legend was to the true story of Creation and the Flood. He saw no reason not to accept their name for the Creator God. Knowing *Thakur Jiu* was the God they had forsaken centuries earlier, the Santal responded immediately to

Skrefsrud's explanation of the gospel. Soon he was baptizing about eighty people each day. During his ministry, Skrefsrud saw fifteen thousand of the Santal people commit their lives to Christ, and during the next few decades at least eighty-five thousand more became Christians.[132]

The Mbakas of the Bantu tribe in central Africa came even closer to the biblical account in their ancient legends. They believed that *Koro*, the Creator, delivered a word to their forefathers that he had already sent his Son into the world to accomplish something wonderful for humanity. Later the forefathers turned away from the truth about *Koro's* Son and eventually forgot what he did for mankind. Since the time of "the forgetting," many generations have longed to rediscover the truth, but all they could learn was that messengers would eventually come to restore the forgotten knowledge to them. This occurred when Ferdinand Rosenau came to preach the gospel to them in the early 1920s.[133]

In the hill country of Ethiopia are several million people who, though divided by many tribes, share a belief in a benevolent being they call *Magano*—omnipotent Creator of all. One of the tribes, the Gedeo, comprise over five hundred thousand people. Though the Gedeo treated *Magano* with profound reverence, they sacrificed to an evil being they called *Sheit'an*. When a group of Gedeo were asked why they sacrificed to *Sheit'an* rather than *Magano*. They replied that, though they had no love for *Sheit'an*, they did not enjoy close enough ties with *Magano* to allow them to be done with *Sheit'an*.

One Gedeo man, however, did seek a personal response from *Magano*. Warrasa Wange, of the royal tribe, asked *Magano* to reveal himself to the Gedeos. Wange began having visions of two white-skinned strangers who would come and build shiny-roofed houses. They would bring a message from *Magano*. Then in a dream Wange saw himself remove the center pole of his house and carry it out of town and plant it in the earth next to one of the shiny-roofed houses. Since the center pole stood for a man's very life, Wange understood

---

132 Ibid., 35–39.
133 Ibid., 59.

this to mean that when the men come, he must identify with them, their message, and with *Magano* who would send them.

Eight full years passed until one day in 1948, Canadians Albert Brant and Glen Cain arrived as missionaries to the Gedeo. Ever vigilant, Warrasa Wange immediately noticed these white strangers who had arrived among them and began asking questions. Several decades later there were two hundred churches among the Gedeos, each averaging over two hundred members.[134]

In 1795 near Rangoon, Burma, an English diplomat appeared among the Karen tribe. The Karen asked him if he was the messenger who was supposed to bring them a book like their forefathers lost long ago. They explained that the book's author was *Y'wa*, the Supreme God, and that the lost book would set them free from oppression.

The diplomat said he had no acquaintance with the god *Y'wa*, and he left the Karen deeply disappointed. One hundred and seventy-five years passed. Teachers called *bukhos* arose among the Karen, reminding them that the ways of *Y'wa* and the ways of *nats* (evil spirits) were not the same. One day, said the *bukhos*, the Karen would return fully to the ways of *Y'wa*. In the meantime, they taught that *Y'wa* was eternal, the Creator, omnipotent, omniscient.

They also told a Creation story. It is unknown how their story contains such similarities to the biblical account, since they had enjoyed no access to the Bible. Here is a summary:

> When Y'wa made Tha-nai and Ee-u, he placed them
> in a garden, saying, "In the garden I have made for
> you seven different kinds of trees, bearing seven kinds
> of fruit. One is not good to eat, if you eat, you will
> become old, you will sicken, you will die. Eat and
> drink with care. Once in seven days I will visit you."
> After a time, Mu-kaw-lee (Satan) came to the man and
> woman and asked why they were there and what they
> ate. The couple said their Lord Y'wa had placed them
> there and they pointed out the foods. They also showed
> him the fruit that would kill them if they ate. Mu-kaw-

---

134 Ibid., 56–58.

lee contradicted Y'wa. He said if they ate, they would possess miraculous powers and would be able to ascend to heaven. Ee-u lingered near the tree, eventually succumbed to temptation, and then gave to Tha-nai to eat. When Mu-kaw-lee learned of it, he laughed. Y'wa came to visit and knew they had eaten the forbidden fruit. He told them they would grow sick and die; he pronounced a curse upon them and left. So they turned to Mu-kaw-lee and he became their master.[135]

In 1817 an American missionary named Adoniram Judson arrived in Rangoon, Burma. In time he translated the Bible into Burmese. One day a Karen man arrived at Judson's door looking for work. His name was Ko Thah-byu, and he was a former criminal who had killed close to thirty men.[136]

As Ko heard snippets of the gospel, it began to penetrate his mind. He suddenly realized that this was surely the book of *Y'wa* for which his people had been waiting for centuries. Quickly enrolling in the missionary school, Ko learned to read and began devouring the Scriptures. Being the first Karen to learn of the lost book, he knew it was his responsibility to proclaim it to every Karen who would listen.

When the missionaries decided to travel farther into Burma, Ko begged to go with them. At every Karen village he preached the gospel, and sometimes the entire village responded in faith. The missionaries became besieged with invitations from numerous Karen villages to come and tell them more from the Book of *Y'wa*.

Two hundred miles to the north another missionary arrived and also began preaching to the Karen to the same ecstatic response. Meanwhile Ko Thah-byu was so determined to tell his people the truth that he scarcely took time to rest. Within years he died from his labors, but he was content. A spiritual harvest rarely equaled in history had taken place.[137]

---

135 Ibid., 78–79.
136 Francis Mason, *The Karen Apostle* (Boston: Gould & Lincoln, 1861), 12.
137 Richardson, *Eternity in Their Hearts*, 90–92.

CHAPTER FIVE

# God: Picketing Peg for the Soul

ONCE THOSE OF OTHER CULTURES KNOW how to identify the God of the Bible, they want to learn more about the nature of this supreme Creator. What is he like? What are his powers? For what offenses does he punish, and what type of curses does he levy? Does he have any faults or weaknesses? What can he do to assuage the needs and crises they regularly face?

Translator Neil Anderson was working on Genesis 1 for the Folopa people of Papua New Guinea. He needed to describe God as Creator, but helpers Hapele and Isa could offer no word in their language for "create."

One day Anderson was invited by the men of the village to accompany them on a hunting trip. He roughed it in the jungle for several days with the Folopa hunters, eating such delicacies as boar brains and roasted grubs. Anderson asked exactly where they got the grubs.

A man named Kima answered, *"Akaoni o foe kaaratapo."* Anderson already knew the verb for "to begin" was *kaatapo*. Now it was being used with a *"ra"* in the middle, which seemed to make the word mean "to cause to begin." Kima was saying that a certain species of beetle creates the grubs or cause the grubs to begin. The Folopa word for God was *Koto*. Anderson added *"ne"* to indicate God was doing the action, then added *"ra"* in the middle of the verb, changing it from "to begin" to "to cause to begin." After adding a few other words, he stated in Folopa, "In the beginning God caused the ground and the sky to come into being." The listeners nodded in unison. What he said made sense in their language.[138]

In another situation Kano, a tribesman assisting with the Wantoat language, heard translator Don Davis read Genesis 1:2: "And the Spirit of God was hovering over the waters."

"If God's Spirit was there," said Kano, "where was God's dead body?"

Davis was taken aback. *Why would he ask such a thing?* Kano explained that their tribe believed that a spirit is never separated from its owner until death. So it was logical that if God's Spirit was separate, God's body must have died. Clearly a modification had to be made so that other tribespeople wouldn't assume the same thing. The translator decided to indicate in the verse the eternal nature of God and his Spirit. He used the expression, "God's ever-ever Spirit."

Kano's dark eyes opened wide in astonishment when he read about a God who has lived forever and about his ever-living Spirit. The concept of a deity who has always lived and will always go on living had never occurred to him. Young Kano's sheer excitement at this truth took a while to subside.[139]

Of course, part of the Creation narrative includes the introduction of sin and rebellion against God. It is interesting to note that there are hundreds of African myths about Creation and about the Supreme Being's extreme withdrawal due to human misbehavior.[140]

After the first sin occurred, Genesis records that cherubim were placed outside the Garden of Eden to guard against anyone eating from the tree of life. An earlier effort in a Tonga language had portrayed angels as those who are appointed to guard God. This whole concept had to be debunked because it communicated the idea that God was so fearful of Satan that he needed bodyguards for protection. Another misconception which had to be corrected among the

---

138 Neil Anderson, *In Search of the Source: A First Encounter with God's Word*, with Hyatt Moore (Portland, OR: Multnomah, 1992), 26–28.
139 Hefley, *Searchlight on Bible Words*, 127.
140 Raimo Harjula, "Theology as Service in Africa," *Pro Veritate* 11, no. 5 (November 1972): 19.

Tonga was the idea that after expelling Adam and Eve from the garden, God remained behind to live it up for a while.[141]

It is interesting to note, however, that even biblically illiterate tribespeople are able to sometimes see without assistance the implications of how being created in God's image relates to sin. Translator Dan Shaw was discussing with Samo tribesmen the passage in Genesis 9 in which God warns humans that it is because they are made in his image that they are not to shed the blood of fellow humans.

A Samo tribesman immediately blurted out, "You mean to say that God doesn't want us going on cannibal raids?" The tribesman went on to explain that their government's arguments against cannibalism were not very convincing, but this stuff about God's image really made sense.[142]

What metaphors are used to describe God in various languages?

One of the Folopa terms for God is *Bete of Betes*. A person might say, "Let's get to the *bete* (source) of our disagreement." Another way the word is used is in reference to people who have tapped into something that gives them power or self-sufficiency. Translator Neil Anderson says that in describing God as the *Bete of Betes* the Folopas began to understand his all-encompassing sufficiency. This term seemed an important one in explaining the Creator God.

As in Psalms, in many cultures God is referred to with other powerful metaphors. The Xhosas describe God as *ingubo*, a sheepskin mantle in which one wraps oneself on a cold evening.[143] There was a problem for a translator when he came to Hebrews 6:19, where it refers to God as a firm and secure "anchor for the soul." The Mossi people, living on the fringes of the Sahara, did not even know what a boat was. They did, however, know a lot about managing livestock, sometimes securing them with stakes they called "picketing pegs." So the translator presented God as the "picketing peg for the soul."[144]

Another tribe in a landlocked region had no way of picturing how God could be a steadfast anchor for souls. Translators substituted *isomo* (center pole) for "anchor." The center pole supports the

---

141 Wendland, *The Cultural Factor*, 63.
142 D. Shaw, *Transculturation*, 67.
143 Sanneh, *Translating the Message*, 196.
144 Wendland, *The Cultural Factor*, 120.

entire roof of a traditional village house. With a solid center pole, a house will neither shift or sway, and when storms strike, it will not collapse.[145]

An additional biblical word picture is the comparison of Christ to a cornerstone. This New Testament culture was one in which the cornerstone served as a foundational reference point supporting an entire structure. But the Samo people, living in lowland swamps, do not use cornerstones. They start with corner posts which serve as primary props for rafters. A critical moment in house construction is the moment when a ridge pole is laid across the lattice work of rafters. These rafters rest on beams, which in turn rest on corner posts placed in the ground. But it is the tightly secured ridge pole that gives the entire structure its stability and strength. Thus, the *ridge pole* becomes the cultural equivalent of the Apostle Paul's "cornerstone." We are the rafter slats, and Christ is our "Ridge Pole," holding the spiritual house, the church, together.[146]

For Middle Easterners, comparing God to a shepherd pictures a protector, a provider, one who looks carefully after his sheep. However, among some Nigerian peoples, this is not an apt metaphor, because only the very young or the insane tend sheep.[147]

In Melanesia and Polynesia an economic trading partner often becomes a man's closest and most trusted friend. One will tell this friend things he will not even tell his wife. What a powerful analogy this is to use in describing the One who "sticks closer than a brother" (Prov 18:24).

However, the ideas of love and forgiveness are difficult to translate in some languages. In central Papua New Guinea, the only expression one translator could identify which would communicate God's forgiveness was, "God doesn't hang up jawbones."[148] When the people there used to kill others in battle, they hung up the jawbones in triumph. Presumably this expression meant that God is not one who holds grudges, kills out of spite, or takes pleasure in cruelty.

---

[145] D. Shaw, *Transculturation*, 50.
[146] David Hesselgrave and Edward Rommen, *Contextualization: Meanings, Methods, and Models* (Grand Rapids: Baker Book House, 1989), 64.
[147] Mayers, *Christianity Confronts Culture*, 231.
[148] Nida and Reyburn, *Meaning across Cultures*, 1.

The idea of God's love and reconciliation toward humanity must be communicated accurately. In one language, missionaries used a particular word for reconciliation for years. Finally they realized that the use of this term suggested clearly that the person taking the initiative in reconciliation—God—was admitting his own guilt in causing the initial estrangement.[149]

In some peasant societies, people understand the love and forgiveness of the father in the parable of the prodigal son, but they see it from a different perspective than Westerners. When the father runs to meet the returning son and kisses him, we in the West assume that he is so excited to see his son that he runs to him. However, in a peasant culture it would be beneath his dignity to run out of excitement. Kenneth Bailey explains that this father would run only in order to protect his son from the village urchins, rabid dogs, and others who may harass the ragged returnee to the point where he may lose his resolve.[150]

Lawrence Reid was trying to translate the idea that "God is love" into the Bontoc language. He'd learned various Bontoc words for love, but they seemed either far too limited in scope or they had strong sensual overtones. Reid's assistant described the word *layad*, and it seemed to have potential, but its meaning was quite broad. Besides meaning "love," it also meant "like" and "want." However, it seemed the best of the lot, so Reid decided to use it.

Then Reid ran into another roadblock. He found that in Bontoc the word "love" could not be used as a noun. He must either say "God has love" or "God loves." He chose the latter form. Next he began sifting through dozens of verbal connectors to find the most suitable. *Lolomyad* was a possibility, but it often refers to a young man's love for his lady friend and may have immoral implications. Using another verbal prefix and reduplication of the first syllable to indicate a continuous aspect, he finally settled on *inal-ayad*. Thus "God is love" (1 John 4:8,16) was translated "*Inal-ayad si Dios*," literally meaning "God is continually loving on and on."[151]

---

149 Ibid., 2.
150 Kenneth Bailey, *Poet and Peasant and Through Peasant Eyes: A Literary-cultural Approach to the Parables in Luke* (Grand Rapids: Eerdmans, 1983), 181–82.
151 Hefley, *Searchlight on Bible Words*, 129.

The Tila Chol Indians were determined that the God of the Bible did not love them; he only pitied them. They did use the word "love" in their human relations but refused to apply it to God. They would always substitute *punt'an* (pity) for *c'uxbin* (love).

One day a translator was drafting 1 John with her translation helper, Alfonso. She was surprised when Alfonso read 1 John 3:1, "*Noj cabal mi' c'uxbinonla lac Ch'u-jutyat*" (Very much he loves us, our holy Father). He had not used the word for "pity."

The translator reminded him that Tila Chols had always said that God can only pity humans.

Alfonso admitted this was true but added, "Then we did not understand about God's love for us. Now I have experienced God's love . . . I know this is the right way to say it, because God *does* love us. The others will come to know, too, that very much he loves us, our holy Father."[152]

The Chacabo Indians of northern Bolivia have an unusual way of declaring mastery or excellence. A man known for his running ability is called *habati ibo* (an owner of running). Linguists Gilbert and Marian Prost used the phrase in Bible translation. A priest became an "owner of worship." They wondered how to express "God is love," since in the framework of the Chacabo language, "love" cannot meaningfully function as a noun. They decided to use the ownership concept. "God is love" became "God is the owner of loving." Being interpreted, this implies, "God is supreme expert at loving."[153]

"God is love" has, in fact, been translated in a number of different ways:

St. Lucian Creole: "Love is the character of God."[154]

Jur Modo (southern Sudan): "God is what is in the middle of love."[155]

Tetelcingo Nahuatl: "God is a Lover."[156]

Orizaba Nawati (roughly): "God is all, pure love."[157]

---

152 Ibid., 130.
153 Ibid., 130–31.
154 David Frank, email message to author, May 2, 2002.
155 Andrew Persson, email message to author, May 2, 2002.
156 David Tuggy, email message to author, April 30, 2002.
157 Ibid.

Manding: "If you say God, you say love."[158]

Rachel Saint and Catherine Peeke learned from legends that the Waorani viewed God as a frightful, angry deity. One story told of a Waorani tiger man who went up to see what heaven is like. God became enraged at him and heaved him out.

When Rachel remarked about the dimples on the ears of a new baby, she heard another myth. "We all have these defects," said a Waorani friend. "It is because of God—when we were living in heaven God became furious at them and said, 'You're always going to do bad anyway!' Then he threw them out to be born on the earth."

However, when Saint and others translated the Scriptures for the Waorani, the tribespeople learned from "God's Carving" that God was not an angry, murderous deity. Today there are Christian Waoranis who are living examples of love and harmony because of a God of love.[159]

Once a people become finally convinced that the Creator God cares for them, they are introduced to the fact that they can actually become intimate friends with this God. When missionaries introduce the practice of prayer to a people, their first question tends to be, in effect, "What do we call God? On what level is the relationship?"

While working through the Gospel of Mark in the Rotokas language, Irwin and Jackie Firchow considered several possible renderings of "Abba, Father," in Mark 14:36.

Finally their language helper brightened. "How about '*Apa, Aite*'?" he said.

The Firchows knew *aite* meant "daddy," but *apa* puzzled them. Was *apa* just "abba" in Rotokas? To their surprise and relief they found that the word is actually a Rotokan appeal for help. So the translation of "*Apa, Aite*" could be understood as "Help me, Daddy," an intimate appeal to a personal God.[160]

In some cultures, addressing God as "heavenly Father" may not imply either warmth or intimacy. The cultural status of a father to a child in such cultures is not close. In fact, in some Melanesian

---

158 Fritz Goerling, email message to author, April 29, 2002.
159 Hefley, *Searchlight on Bible Words*, 131.
160 Ibid., 128.

societies, it is the mother's brother who is often closest to the children.[161] Might it be appropriate, then, to allow believers in such a culture to address God as "Uncle" instead of "Father"?

Neil Anderson had been using the word *hoso* for "prayer" in Folopa. As another linguist checked Anderson's translation for accuracy, he wondered if *hoso* was the most appropriate word. *Hoso* seemed to mean an incantation of some sort. Anderson had considered another word, *moma*, but the word seemed too closely associated with contacting spirits.

As the linguist questioned the Folopa further, he learned that people repeated particular incantations, depending upon what they wanted. They would say one *hoso* when they planted yams, another when they built a fence, and so on. When the linguist asked if the incantations worked, the Folopa said, "Who knows? It was the only way."

The linguist asked if people still did it. The Folopa answered, "Some do. Others pray." Actually, they replied, "Some *hoso*. Others *hoso*." It was only the voice inflection, the focused look, the you-know-what-I-mean nod that conveyed that prayer was somehow different.

The linguist decided to find out more about the word *moma*. The Folopa explained that *moma* was a speech addressed to powerful spirit beings, including the spirits of the departed. It was more spontaneous and adaptable, not formulaic, like the *hoso*. The power of *hoso* was in the litany, the power of the *moma* was in the spirit to whom it was addressed. *Moma* seemed to fit the true concept of prayer better than did *hoso*. Anderson and his translator friend reasoned that though *moma* had been used by the Folopa perhaps to contact evil spirits, there was no reason why it could not now be used to speak to God. The concept of *moma* was not evil in itself. And certainly it fit Christian theology that the power of *moma* was not in the words prayed but in the one addressed.[162]

To the English speaker, "to ask" and "to promise" have completely different, almost opposite, meanings. In the Toura language

---

161 D. Shaw, *Transculturation*, 74.
162 Anderson, *In Search*, 118–24.

of Cote d'Ivoire (also known as Ivory Coast), however, the same expression is used for both. In this language there are three ways of asking somebody for something:

(1) One Toura word is generally used when the person asking strongly suspects that the other party is not well disposed toward him or his family and that a special effort of politeness must be made to coax him into giving. Obviously the Bible doesn't portray God as someone who is against us and from whom we must beg.

(2) The second expression is literally "to call for giving." This is used only when asking a gift from a person with whom one is not in a giving-receiving relationship. This would imply that God is like a stranger to us, one who normally is not close enough to share with us.

(3) To clarify the third term, the translator asked the cotranslator what a child would say if he went confidently to his father to ask for something. The cotranslator said that the child would "tell him the matter." For example, if he wanted bread, he would tell him the bread matter, etc.

The third term was the expression the translator decided to use in verses such as John 15:7: "If you remain in me and my words remain in you, ask me whatever matter you wish and it will be given you." Finally he learned that it was the particular context which determined whether a Toura interpreted the expression as a request or a promise. In other words, if a superior is speaking to an inferior, then "to tell a matter" means to promise. If an inferior is addressing a superior, then it constitutes a request.[163]

When translating Luke 11:11, Neil Anderson read aloud to the Folopa: "Which of you fathers, if your son asks for a fish, will give him a snake instead?"

They stared at Neil blankly. "Why not give him a snake?" they asked. After all, a large snake was a rare treat that could feed a whole family. But a fish in Folopa territory was very small and would barely qualify as a snack.

---

163 Translation Treasures, *In Other Words*, August 1975, 7.

In the Jewish culture, snakes were considered unclean, totally unfit to eat, while fish was a staple of their diet. For the Folopas, Anderson could have justifiably switched the translation to read: "Which of you fathers, if your son asks for a snake, will give him a fish instead?"

Instead he decided to render the verse: "If your son is hungry and he wants a fish, you wouldn't toss him a live snake of the kind that when it bites people they die." This may not have been the perfect translation, but the main point of the verse was not snakes and fish anyway, but the fact that, whatever good earthly fathers give their children, God is a Father who gives infinitely more.[164]

One crucial aspect of prayer is actually believing that God will provide what we need in response to our requests. God often wants to lead us into "a land of milk and honey," and we don't even seek it. God's all-sufficiency is clearly pictured in a Chewa equivalent for "land of milk and honey." It reads literally, "the land of 'what can a child cry for?'" In other words, a child need never cry there because the parent constantly gives the child everything it requires.[165]

Fear can rule the Christian who does not pray. It's interesting how the Chewa language expresses the power of fear. In Chewa, a verse that reads, "His heart will utterly melt with fear," reads instead, "He will be broken off in his knees."[166]

When we're really trusting God as our deeply caring parent, we don't have to be ruled by worry or fear. Anxiety in Navajo is expressed vividly by a word meaning "that which pricks and irritates," like a pin jabbing flesh. Thus 1 Peter 5:7 reads, "The things that are continually sticking into you, turn them over to me, for I am interested in you and am caring about you."[167]

That doesn't mean that life isn't difficult and demanding at times. When Jesus said, "Come to me, all you who are weary and burdened" (Matt 11:28), he may have been thinking of the Mazatecs. From infancy most Mazatecs are expected to carry many physical burdens. They use a long rope with a wide band in the middle

---

164 Anderson, *In Search*, 128–29.
165 Wendland, *The Cultural Factor*, 104.
166 Ibid., 130.
167 Hefley, *Searchlight on Bible Words*, 36–37.

section. The ends of the rope are tied around the pack to be carried, the band is placed across the top of the carrier's head, and the pack hangs down his back from the top of his head. Mazatecs are extremely aware of the difference between a bad (hard) burden and a good (easy) burden. Bad burdens have sharp edges which cut into their backs, or moving parts which tend to throw them off balance as they walk. A good burden feels lighter and is shaped to their backs. Mazatecs had no word similar to "yoke," so translators decided to render Matthew 11:29, "my carrying rope is easy and my burden is light." Mazatecs now understood clearly what Jesus was saying.

CHAPTER SIX

# Family Affairs

IN MANY CULTURES, RELATIONSHIPS TO EXTENDED FAMILY and other loved ones are much more closely bound than in the West. The Bible translation process uncovers some ideas on community from which we Westerners may well learn.

For example, in traditional African culture every person's greatest responsibility by far is to one's family and, if need be, everything is sacrificed for the sake of family. This sense of community is so tightly knit in a given village that the breakdown of one relationship is enough to throw the whole group into chaos. So the damage evil can do is constantly on the minds of villagers, and they speak out immediately when wrongs are committed so a score can be settled or reconciliation made before greater harm can be done. While we thrive on competition, we must also admit that when competition becomes ruthless, it can reap destruction and feed grudges. The African culture plays down competition, focusing more on cooperation and mutual reciprocity.[168]

Though family is also extremely important in the Folopa culture of New Guinea, women have not always been treated with respect.

---

168 Monica Wilson, *Religion and the Transformation of Society* (Cambridge: Cambridge University Press, 1971), 139.

*Bete* is one of the most common words in the Folopa language. As mentioned in the previous chapter, its primary meaning is "source." As Neil Anderson translated Genesis into the Folopa language, he explained to the Folopas that woman was created out of man. Hapele, the translation helper, remarked, "So, the *bete* of woman is man."

In Folopa culture, women are the chief burden-bearers of society; beyond this, their roles have been greatly restricted. However, as word got around that woman was made from man, they gained a new status, and their relationships with men were improved. A seed of dignity had been sown which soon began to bear fruit.[169]

Occasionally customs of Scripture can be misunderstood in other cultures. Husband/wife relationships with their in-laws are extremely crucial in many cultures and must be maintained with the greatest courtesy. In Ruth 2:18 we find that Ruth carried extra barley to her mother-in-law but "gave her what she had left over after she had eaten enough." But in the Chewa culture giving a loved one *mkute*, "food remaining from the night before," is considered very selfish. Though we view Ruth as very giving, in traditional African society anything they think smacks of greed or gluttony is looked upon as particularly abhorrent.[170]

Genesis 2:24 reads, "A man will leave his father and mother and be united to his wife." But in the Tonga culture of Zambia, a newly married couple traditionally live in the home of or close by the husband's parents. Are they disobeying this guideline of Scripture? Translators concluded they are not, believing that the leaving of father and mother does not necessarily mean geographical separation as much as the shift of central emotional attachment from parents to one's spouse.[171]

Speaking of marriage, the Tzeltal believers of Mexico could not understand Paul's admonition to refrain from marriage if one desires to serve God more faithfully. In their family-centered culture, young people did not really settle down to serve God wholeheartedly until

---

169 Anderson, *In Search*, 53–54.
170 Wendland, *The Cultural Factor*, 176.
171 Ibid., 96.

*Family Affairs*

they *did* get married.[172] Until then, they tended to be rather carefree and egocentric.

In some languages, familial relationships are reflected even in the colloquial expressions used on a daily basis. For example, Paul's exclamation in Romans 7:24, "What a wretched man I am!" would be rendered in the Tonga language, "Mercy me! I am my own younger brother" (I have no one to look to in this crisis).[173]

For Folopas, father-son relationships constitute strong bonds, particularly unique between a father and his youngest son. There is even a separate term for the youngest: "the milk-stops baby." In Genesis when Joseph was testing his brothers and asked them to bring the youngest brother, Benjamin, the Folopa identified with the great struggle Jacob had in risking the life of his youngest. They also understood the raw courage Judah exhibited when he offered his life in return for the boy's. When, finally, Joseph revealed himself to his brothers and they were reconciled, the Folopa were greatly moved. One older man looked up at the translator and said, "We are dying of the deliciousness of these words."[174]

Though community is a vital concept especially in many Majority World cultures, Don Richardson writes of a strange aberration in his popular book, *Peace Child*. When he and his wife went as missionary translators to the Sawi tribe of Papua, Indonesia they found a culture in which treachery and hatred were prized and even nurtured.

For example, wives might be punished with an arrow through an arm or leg, and children of the Sawi tribe were taught to strike back when parents disciplined them. They were trained to get their way by sheer force of violence and temper and were goaded constantly to take *otaham* (revenge) every time they were hurt or insulted. In fact, with similarly hostile tribes all around them, the Sawi knew that unless the young were taught this way, they'd quickly become the prey of enemies.[175]

Even more insidious, the most treacherous Sawi were the most admired. The epic stories of the southwest Irian Jayans were stories in

---

172 Nida and Reyburn, *Meaning across Cultures*, 31.
173 Wendland, *The Cultural Factor*, 153.
174 Anderson, *In Search*, 81–83.
175 Don Richardson, *Peace Child* (Glendale, CA: Regal Books, 1974), 186.

which those of neighboring tribes were deceived by outward friendliness and generosity only to be brutally murdered when their guard was down. This practice was called *tuwi asonai man* (fattening a pig for slaughter).

Thus when Don Richardson began learning Sawi and told them the gospel story, it was not Jesus and his sacrifice that won their admiration but Judas, the "ultimate Super-*sawi*." Richardson was appalled.[176] How could he convince these people that it was Jesus, not Judas, who was the hero of the story?

As the months passed, the Richardsons witnessed almost constant violence, sometimes among the Sawi, but mostly feud-fighting between tribes. Don found his urgings for peace to be useless. Even if tribes agreed to a treaty, their philosophy of treachery would make the treaty a perfect setup for deception.

Then one day some Sawi leaders came to see Richardson with the claim, "Tomorrow we are going to sprinkle cool water (make peace) on each other."

Was it another sham? The next morning a Sawi father walked toward the neighboring village in tears, carrying a baby son. His wife followed behind, wailing out her loss. Then the man hesitated; he could not give up his child. He turned back. A fellow tribesman went into his hut and picked up his only son and walked the same path. He gave it to a chosen man of the enemy tribe to be his own. Then, in turn, a man from the other tribe gave his son to the tribesman to belong to him. All the members of the respective villages laid their hands on the newly adopted children, thus pledging peace. This act was the ceremony of the *tarop tim* (peace child).

Shortly after this ceremony, a clash developed between members of the two tribes. Before violence could erupt, someone ran and brought one of the two peace children, crying, "I plead the peace child." Violence was averted. Richardson suddenly understood the concept; if a man would actually give his own son to his enemies, that man could be trusted.

An idea began forming in Richardson's mind that he believed was from God. He gathered the men of the Sawi village together and said,

---

176 Ibid., 177–78.

"You and your ancestors are not the only ones who found that peace required a peace child. *Myao Kodon* (God), the Spirit whose message I bear, has declared the same thing—true peace can never come without a peace child. Never!"

Richardson went on to explain that because *Myao Kodon* wanted humans to find peace with him and with each other, he chose a once-for-all *tarop* child good enough and strong enough to establish peace forever.

"Whoever did he choose?" asked one of the Sawi. "Did he give another man's son or his own?"

"He gave his own," replied Richardson. "God had only one Son to give, a beloved Son, but . . . he gave him anyway!"

Richardson read John 3:16 to the men.

One of them said, "Is this the Yesus you've been telling us about? You said a friend betrayed him—if Yesus was a *Tarop*, it was very wrong to betray him. We have a name for that. We call it *tarop gaman*. It's the worst thing anyone could do."

"You're right," Richardson said, "Despising the *Tarop* child of God is the worst thing anyone can do. *Myao Kodon* knew beforehand that men would despise and murder the Peace Child he sent to them, but *Myao Kodon* loves us so much that he gave him anyway . . . And the ones who shed the blood of Yesus actually provided a *raendep*, (an atonement) to quench God's anger against men . . . *Myao Kodon* was so *maraviap*, (ingenious) that the worst men could do only furthered his purpose."

The Sawi men sat in awe as they heard these words.

"In the case of a Sawi *tarop*," Richardson reasoned, "you receive him bodily into your home . . . But in the case of God's *Tarop*, no one receives him bodily."

"Then how can we receive him?" asked one of the men.

"You receive *Myao Kodon's* Peace Child by welcoming his Spirit into your hearts. Then he becomes your Provider and Protector . . . You will actually enter into a *hauwat*, (name exchange) relationship with the God of heaven and earth. He will link your names with the name of his Son and accept you for his sake."

There was stillness in the manhouse as this message sank in, then a steady murmur as the men began discussing this amazing new truth.[177]

In the weeks to follow, two of the young men of the village gave their hearts over to Yesus, but none of the tribal leaders did so. Then finally a respected warrior named Hato stood up in the manhouse. Hato's chest heaved with emotion. His voice was low as he turned to Richardson. "Your words make my liver tremble" (You have aroused longing within me). His voice choked out, "*Myao Kodon fidasir Tarop Tim fasi fofadivi*" (I want to receive the Peace Child of God).[178]

More Sawis turned to the Peace Child, but some horrible customs remained. One custom was called *gefam ason* (touching the stench). When a Sawi died, relatives kept constant vigil around the unburied, rotting corpse for nine days. As the stench grew worse, the wailing grew louder. Finally a relative would plunge a fist into the decaying body cavity, then, with that dripping hand, would eat some freshly cooked sago bread.

Richardson heard a grief-stricken woman wailing in anguish, asking when the "words of *remon*," would come and free them from death. He was told that *remon* was how a caterpillar escapes death by metamorphosing into a moth. The words of *remon* hinged on a legend that long ago humans possessed the power to live endlessly:

> A lizard and a karasu bird had an argument. The lizard, as symbol of *remon*, claimed people should remain free from the power of death. The bird, because it dies so readily, symbolized death. It insisted that humans should become subject to death. The lizard kept repeating "*rimi! rimi!* renew! renew!" but the bird kept saying "*sanay! sanay!* decay! decay!" Finally the lizard caved in to the will of the bird and humans began to die. It was not known why the lizard did this,

---

177  Ibid., 211–19.
178  Ibid., 233.

but ancestors had claimed that someday the words of *remon* would return and death would end.[179]

Richardson believed that hopeless customs such as *gefam ason* grew out of the universal human feeling that ends not attainable by force or ordinary persuasion can be won by subjecting oneself to extreme humiliation or mortification. He wanted to communicate to the Sawi the Bible's answer for prisoners of this compulsion— the humiliation and death of Christ on our behalf. He wanted them to realize that Christ's resurrection offers the only hope of *remon* humans can ever know.

Richardson summoned the Sawi Christians and again described the resurrection of Yesus. He also explained that Yesus had raised others from death and had claimed to be the Resurrection and the Life.

"His words are the words of *remon*!" said Richardson. "They bring you first the *remon* of your inner man through the Holy Spirit inside you, to be followed, according to the promise of Scripture, by the *remon* of your bodies on the Day of Christ. If you believe Yesus' words, do you still need to practice *gefam ason* on the bodies of your loved ones?"

Hato, the first leader who believed, stood up. "Thank God you told us that," he said. "Now we can quit that ugly practice. When it comes my turn to die," he told his relatives, "let my body rot in peace. If you carry out *gefam ason*, it will mean you really don't believe the promise of *remon* in Yesus."[180]

It was through these providentially ordained redemptive analogies that Don Richardson saw God transform brutal relationships and bring peace to thousands of Sawi families.

---

179 Ibid., 260–61.
180 Ibid., 262–63.

# CHAPTER SEVEN

# And the Father Said, "*Supo*"

In most cases, when Bible translators begin their work, the first book they translate is one of the four Gospels. The brief and straightforward Gospel of Mark is often the choice, but preferences of translators vary.

Don and Launa Davis were translating the birth of Christ from Matthew's Gospel into the Wantoat language. When they came to the verse about the Magi from the east, they had a problem. The Wantoats did not use the terms "north," "south," "east," or "west." The closest they came to this was saying "upriver or downriver, or up mountains or down river gorges."

The best tentative translation the Davises could come up with was "the Wise Ones came from where the sun comes up." This did not suggest the fact that the Magi came from a far distance, so the Davises kept their ears open for a better term.

Finally, at a Bible study a Wantoat read about the Magi and said, "What this really means is '*Guzitde yapiiatanga Jerusalem apbiy*' (They came to Jerusalem from the sun's source)." This rendering included not only direction but the idea of great distance as well.[181]

---

181 Translation Treasures, *In Other Words*, December 1977, 6.

The Gospel of John opens, not with the birth of Christ, but by portraying Jesus as the Word. Translating the Greek for "word" (*logos*) is in itself a daunting challenge—the Liddell and Scott lectionary allegedly lists more than seventy different renderings.[182]

Translator Wesley Thiesen was trying to translate John 1:1 into the Bora language. "Word" and "mouth" are the same word in the Bora language, but equating God with mouth would make no sense to them. Thiesen considered the meaning of the Greek *logos*. A primary definition contained the idea of revelation—the revealer of God. He and his language assistant wondered about using the word for "cause to know." But this introduced another problem. If they used "cause to know," they'd have to use the inanimate form "it." "It" was obviously unacceptable when referring to the person of Christ. Finally the two decided upon the phrase, "the One who causes to know." Their rendition of the complete verse became: "Before everything began, there was the One who had the Word that caused to know about God. He was with God. He was God."[183]

Eileen Kilpatrick worked among the Avokayas of the Sudan. The typical term for "word" in Avokaya was very generic, always referring to speech, and capitalization of it would not serve to personify it. So in John 1:1, instead of writing, "In the beginning was the Word," she took advantage of a particle meaning "the one who . . ." to create a phrase meaning "the one who reveals God." The expression fit perfectly to signal an animate being as the topic without needing to tell the reader that Jesus is the object. It also fit well into the entire prologue of John. Then in John 1:1 she portrayed Jesus as "he who was God's heart," implying his intimate, essential relationship with the Father.[184]

The Mayfields, translators among the Central Cagayan Agta, were puzzling over how to translate the phrase in John 1:1, "And the Word was God [the same essence and nature as God]." One day they heard the Agta people say, "*Itta ya kagittamuy*," when they glimpsed others like them. The Mayfields learned that *kagitta* meant

---

182 Henry Liddell and Robert Scott, *A Greek-English Lexicon* (US: Oxford University Press, 1996).
183 Hefley, *Searchlight on Bible Words*, 126.
184 Eileen Kilpatrick, email message to author, March 6, 2002.

"anything of the same appearance and/or essence as another." Thus, in the Agta language John 1:1 read: "*A kagitta na Namahatu ya uhohugen.*" Translated freely back into English this means: "And the Word was the sameness or equalness of God."[185]

The Apostle John continues in chapter 1 to record that the Word became flesh and tented among us. He was the light of the world, yet the world preferred to remain in darkness. But to those who believed in him he gave the right to become children of God.

To be able to make humans children of God, Jesus had to accept the death penalty humanity deserved. In John 18:11 the English Bible records Christ's statement to Peter: "Shall I not drink the cup the Father has given me?" To the Muinane Indians the "cup" is only a strange item white men use. They use a large, folded leaf to capture water. They also occasionally use a gourd, but only in the context of celebratory dances, not a sorrowful setting such as Christ's death.

Translators also had to make sure that the translation didn't imply to the Muinane that Jesus would conceivably rebel against his Father. The authority of the father in the Muinane culture is undisputed. Thus the translators dropped the cup metaphor and rendered the verse: "Jesus said to Peter . . . 'Do you not know that my Father has commanded that I should suffer? And how can I say "no" to him?'"[186]

A Mazatec Indian was reading this same story surrounding the events before Christ's crucifixion and, at one point, he began chuckling softly. Translator Eunice Pike could not imagine what there was about the crucifixion story that he would find amusing. She thought maybe a translation error had struck him funny.

He'd been reading of Gethsemane, and he read John 18:6 aloud. The Indian reiterated, "When Jesus said, 'I am he,' they drew back and fell to the ground. They could not have done a thing to him without his permission," the man said confidently.

In rendering the scene in which Judas kissed Jesus to identify him to his captors, a Nigerian language required what to Westerners would seem very strange. The Kaje language assistant read of the

---

185 Hefley, *Searchlight on Bible Words*, 58.
186 Translation Treasures, *In Other Words*, July–August 1974.

kiss and immediately reacted against it. He said, "Kaje do not kiss to greet. We would say, 'Judas came and licked Jesus.'"[187] To us, this sounds almost sacreligious, but the Nigerian was dead serious. In his mind, he was correcting an expression which would seem completely ludicrous to his people.

This one whom Judas identified in the garden as a criminal to be arrested was he whom John the Baptist identified as "the Lamb of God, who takes away the sin of the world!" (John 1:29). In some parts of Africa goats are much preferred to sheep as a standard of value and a medium of exchange and could well be substituted in Scripture passages which picture Jesus as a lamb.[188]

This idea is not without precedent. In the Old Testament there is a picture of Christ's atonement in the ritual of the scapegoat. The Dyaks of Borneo enacted a similar ritual that seems to have evolved out of an innate conviction of the need for sins to be absolved.

For the ritual two chickens were selected, both healthy and without blemish. One chicken was killed and its blood sprinkled along the shore of the river. The other chicken was tethered alive to the deck of a small boat. A small lantern was also placed on the boat and lit. Then the villagers filed by the boat, each placing something invisible in it. If asked what was being put in the boat, villagers replied, "*Dosaku*" (My sin). Then the boat was released into the river. If it drifted out of sight, the villagers would shout, "*Selamat! Selamat!*" (We're safe! We're safe!). If it drifted back to shore or capsized, the people lived in fear of retribution for another year.[189]

In Leviticus 16 God commanded a somewhat similar symbolic ceremony to be enacted. On the Day of Atonement, Aaron was to take two male goats and cast lots to find out which was to belong to the Lord and which was to be the scapegoat. The one belonging to God was sacrificed as a sin offering; the other was sent into the desert as a scapegoat, or one meant to bear guilt or blame for the people. The Dyaks used chickens instead of goats and they didn't use

---

187 Translation Treasures, *In Other Words*, March–April 1974, 14.
188 Wendland, *The Cultural Factor*, 62.
189 Richardson, *Eternity in Their Hearts*, 106–7.

a scapegoat, they used a "scapeboat," but how they arrived at an idea so similar to the biblical one we are not certain.

In any case, Christ became the final "scapegoat," taking our sins upon himself. But what was it that pointed us to our need for Christ? Paul reiterates in Galatians that the law of God was our "tutor." Other English translations render the law as our "guardian" or our "custodian" to lead us to Christ. In Chewa society there is no equivalent to this idea. Translators finally decided to use as a substitute the *namkungwi*, a female supervisor overseeing girls' initiation ceremonies. Of course, it is made clear that the law tutored all, not just females, toward faith in Christ.[190]

Sacrifice is not a rare concept in world religions. Wayan Mastra tells of a situation which occurred as he preached the gospel among the Balinese of Indonesia. A distraught woman approached him expressing great unhappiness that her husband and children had become Christians. She was afraid that her ancestors and the deities would punish her family because they no longer brought offerings to the family temples.

Mastra realized that Balinese Hindu burnt and food offerings somewhat resemble Old Testament offerings. He wisely told the woman that Christians already had their final offering which was made at Mount Golgotha in Palestine once and for all in the person of Jesus Christ. God himself actually became human for our sakes. Hence Christians do not have to bring offerings and shed blood anymore because the offering of Jesus Christ was enough. However, Christians, out of a spirit of dedication and love, do voluntarily bring offerings to God in the form of money.

The woman accepted this explanation, placed her trust in Christ, and became one of the most active Christians in Bali.[191]

Following Christ's identification and mock trial, he was condemned to be crucified. One translator read Matthew 27:32 to his language assistant: "They found a man of Cyrene, Simon by name: him they compelled to bear his cross" (KJV).

---

190 Wendland, *The Cultural Factor*, 121.
191 Stott and Coote, *Gospel and Culture*, 367–68.

Abruptly the informant asked, "Did Jesus possess a cross of his own?"

The translator was taken aback. "No, it was not Jesus' personally owned cross. It was the one he was carrying."

To avoid misunderstanding, the translation was rendered: "And they forced Simon to shoulder the cross that Jesus was carrying."[192]

When the Boras of northeastern Peru first heard 1 John 5:6, "This is the one who came by water and blood," the Boras understood that Jesus came in a canoe and was bleeding. They cannot really be blamed for this misunderstanding. Even comparatively knowledgeable Bible students sometimes puzzle over this verse. In any case, translators Wesley and Eva Thiesen changed their translation to read: "Jesus passed through water in baptism and shed his blood in dying."[193]

The idea that Jesus died with criminals, as if he was one of them, must also be communicated. The Hershbergers were unable to translate Mark 15:28, "And [Jesus] was numbered with the transgressors" (KJV). In the Gugu-Yalanji language, they could find no word for "transgressor" and no verb form meaning "to number or classify." However, they did learn that to convey a concept such as this the Gugu-Yalanji people would use a direct quote. So they rendered the verse: "Everyone said, 'He [Jesus] is also bad.'"[194]

In Folopa there is no equivalent word for "crucifixion." A great deal of explanation had to take place before they began to understand what a crucifixion was. A naive translator might have suggested that a more familiar method of death be substituted, such as lynching or drowning. But it is obviously imperative that crucifixion be retained for various reasons, including the fact that Christ's blood had to be shed for sin.

Even when the Folopa finally realized that crucifixion involves hanging or nailing a person on a wooden stake or pole, they misunderstood. They thought Jesus was hung on the cross *after* he was

---

192 Translation Treasures, *In Other Words*, March–April 1974, 14.
193 Hefley, *Searchlight on Bible Words*, 56.
194 Ibid., 56–57.

killed. Then they thought Jesus and the two criminals were all hung on the same cross.

The translator patiently explained that the hanging itself was the means of punishment, one person per cross. He also disclosed that Jesus had spoken some important words while on the cross.

Once they understood it, the crucifixion of Jesus had a much more profound impact on the Folopa than it does on violence-hardened Westerners. At one point the Folopa watched a film about Jesus' life. Though they had been told the portrayal was a pretense by actors, the women erupted with excruciating wails of grief when they saw Jesus being nailed to the cross. They couldn't help reacting this way because Jesus was someone they were coming to trust and truly love.[195]

Occasionally, when there is no word or phrase in a language to express completely a biblical concept, translators must construct a new one or put together words in unique ways. When working with the Washkuk people group, Neal and Martha Kooyers found no word or phrase in their language to express the fact that Jesus died for all. The Washkuk language did have a suffix "-*chi*" that was sometimes added to verb stems to show an action is done for someone else. Though it had never been done, the Kooyers decided to add this suffix to the verb stem "*ha*," meaning "to die."

*Hachi* fit the pattern of the language, but would the people understand? When the Kooyers introduced the word to their language assistant, Budia, he repeated the word several times, not sure if he liked it.

Weeks later, Budia's wife, Mukuchua, returned from a Bible study conducted in the trade language. Martha Kooyers asked what she had heard. She replied, "*Jesus riita ya nona hachi*" (Jesus came to die for us). She'd used the word naturally and easily, and the Kooyers were gratified. Apparently the new word did convey the vital fact that Jesus died for the Washkuks.[196]

Wilfred Douglas, who worked among the Aborigines, was once told by an Aborigine that it was no miracle for Jesus to die and to

---

195 Anderson, *In Search*, 150–51.
196 Hefley, *Searchlight on Bible Words*, 55.

rise again. According to Aborigines, anyone who has a high fever, is unconscious, or extremely weak may be considered "dead." Douglas was forced to clarify exactly what he meant by death.

A Bible translator among the Sierra Chontals of Mexico faced a similar problem. The same word in their language means both "to die" or "to become unconscious." The Chontals thought that devils had tried to murder Jesus, but he fooled them. He was only unconscious, and when the devils were not looking, he awoke and escaped up into heaven. So obviously the Chontals were also not very impressed by Christ's prophecy that he would be dead for three days and then rise (Cf. Mark 9:31). In describing the Crucifixion, the translator had to actually spell out that Christ's heart stopped beating throughout the three days before he rose from the dead.[197]

In order to explain to the Folopas why Jesus was crucified, Neil Anderson knew he would have to discover the word equivalent for "ransom." As he tried to explain to his language helpers the word he was searching for, he seemed to be getting nowhere. Finally, though, one helper said thoughtfully, "We do have something like you describe. It isn't quite the same—it was never used with an enemy, but between clans it's called *duputapo*."

He explained a situation in which a man named Wotale was clearing land for a garden. He warned a woman that a tree he was chopping down might fall on her. She didn't move in time, and she was killed by the falling tree. Her relatives went for their weapons and gathered outside the man's longhouse, demanding Wotale's life. Wotale's clan brothers began spreading valuables out on the ground, objects they would never give up except under great duress. Angry bartering and bickering went on until finally someone from the woman's clan yelled, "*Supo*."

*Supo* means "enough."

The leader of Wotale's house said, "*Duputapo*," and the trade was completed.

Anderson decided to try the word in Scripture. He roughed out a verse: "We were in jeopardy of being killed but Jesus came to make a trade (*duputapo*). He gave up his life instead and we got to go free."

---

197 Ibid., 47.

A tribesman nodded, "*Duputapo*. And God the Father said, '*Supo*.'"

An old man who'd been listening intensely said, "That is hard to believe. Your *duputapo* was a man. In the past we've given a great deal to trade for a clan brother—a great deal. But we've never given a person. And a person could never offer himself!"

He leaned back and said, "We are dying of the deliciousness of this talk."[198]

Greedy white traders, disease, and abysmal poverty had decimated the Machiguengas of Peru, leaving them devoid of hope. Most mothers of the tribe had lost at least three children, and whenever translators Wayne and Betty Snell would leave the tribe for a few weeks, tribespeople would say pessimistically, "We won't be here when you return. We will all be dead."

It is not surprising, therefore, that the first verses of John 14 became a favorite for Machiguenga Christians. It seemed incredible to them that Christ would prepare a place for his children—a comfortable and beautiful house that will never fall down or be consumed by termites, a house for which they will not need to go many days' journey to collect leaves for a roof. And the Machiguengas have found great hope in the promise that even now Jesus is working on their eternal home in heaven.

The first Machiguenga hymn was based on Christ's promise of an eternal home.

> Where my Father lives, there are very, very many houses;
> Where my Father lives, there are very, very many houses;
> If there weren't any, I would have told you.
> I would then have said, "Up high there are no homes."
> Now because I'm going, I'll prepare, I'll prepare for you;
> Houses up high, so that you won't suffer.
> The Lord Jesus said, "I am the trail,
> If you all will follow me, you'll live up high with God."
>
> Chorus:
> I'll return, I'll return;

---

198 Anderson, *In Search*, 159–63.

I'll come back and get you all;
Wherever I am, truly you will be, all of you.[199]

It's great to see hope broadcast in the smiles of new Christians from any culture, but "hope" in the biblical sense is one of the most universally difficult words to translate. Working among the Valiente Indians, translators finally discovered that the idea of "hope in God" is expressed by the phrase meaning, "resting one's mind in God."[200]

In the Buang language, Bruce and Joyce Hooley tentatively settled on a word that meant "to think about and wait for." However, as Bruce reviewed the New Testament translation with Mose, his translation helper, he noticed a construction he'd never noticed before. The normal expression for "thinking" in Buang is *kwa nevo*. However, in the passage at hand, the expression was reversed: *nevo kwa*. Thinking it was an error, Bruce questioned Mose about it.

Mose explained that this was a legitimate Buang word, and it meant excitedly waiting for something to occur. Bruce suggested that this would be a good word for "hope," especially the hope of Christ's return.

"No, that's no good," said Mose. "This word gives the idea of eager expectation, like you felt the other day when you were waiting for the mail to arrive, and you kept getting up and going to the door to look for Yarambing. Isn't his return just a thing that could happen sometime in the distant future?"

But Bruce knew that eager expectation was exactly the idea that needed to be conveyed. By using "*nevo kwa*," the translation conveys accurately the anticipation the Apostle Paul felt when thinking of Christ's return. The honest Mose was implying how faint our hope sometimes becomes as the decades and centuries of waiting pass.[201]

---

199 Hefley, *Searchlight on Bible Words*, 146–47.
200 Sanneh, *Translating the Message*, 197.
201 Translation Treasures, *In Other Words*, April 1977, 4.

CHAPTER EIGHT

# The Road of the Quiet Heart

As Bible translators enter a new culture and begin to translate the gospel into the native language, it becomes strikingly obvious that, universally, the great human search is for inner peace. In Romans 3:17, Paul says of those from all races and backgrounds, "The way of peace they do not know." The Chol language expresses this thought perfectly: "They have not known the road of the quiet heart."[202]

Paul Smith was attempting to translate John 3:16, the ultimate word of peace, into the Chinantec Ojitlan dialect of eastern Mexico. When Smith quoted, "God so loved the world," his language helper asked exactly who that included.

"Oh," said Smith, "this means God loves Chinantecs, Mexicans, foreigners, everybody."

"Then you must say specifically 'God loved *all the people* in the world,'" the Indian concluded. "If you just say 'the world,' Chinantecs will think God loves even the evil in the world."[203]

When Neil Anderson came to John 3:16, he wasn't sure of the right word for "love" in the Folopa language. In conversation with a

---
202 Nida, *God's Word*, 40.
203 Hefley, *Searchlight on Bible Words*, 157.

Folopa woman, Carol, Neil's wife had heard a word that seemed to denote a special feeling. The woman explained how, when her first husband died, it hadn't been heartbreaking because her feelings for him were not strong. But she was very close to her second husband. She told Carol, "I married that one for *koneo*."

Anderson had not considered this word because it was used in so many ways. The Folopa would use the word as a sort of greeting, a farewell, or a term of endearment. Anderson asked his translation assistant, "Would it work if we used the word *koneo* to say God cares so much for the world that he sent his Son?"

"Yes," said the assistant excitedly. "That's exactly the right word." It was the word for simple, pure love.[204]

The Amahuacas of the Amazon basin do not have a precise equivalent for the word "love." The closest expression is "he wants or likes." So, though it sounds understated, the translation of John 3:16 begins, "God wants and likes everybody." The remainder of the verse in Amahuaca reads: "Liking/wanting everyone, God gave us his only Son. He gave us his only Son that all who trust him will not die but will live without ceasing."[205]

Similarly, when Perry and Anne Priest translated John 3:16 into the Siriono language of Bolivia, it seemed as if they would also have to be content with a rather weak expression for God's love. The verse began, "For God strongly liked the people of the world so much . . ."

Then one day they heard a new word, *nyesecua*, and thought it might be their much-sought-after term for supreme love. However their language informant said he rarely felt at ease expressing such an emotion, even to family members. "In fact," he said, "we Sirionos rarely use that word except when we're drunk."

The Priests had no desire to use a drunkard's word in describing God's love, so they promptly laid the word aside. However, new Siriono believers began suggesting, "We should be saying *nyesecua* to God and to each other now that we know Jesus as our Savior."

Perry Priest began puzzling out the issue. "Why would they use the word only when drunk, yet now feel that, as believers, they

---

204 Anderson, *In Search*, 95–96.
205 Hefley, *Searchlight on Bible Words*, 35.

should use it?" Then Perry thought of the scriptural contrast in Ephesians between being filled with wine and being filled with the Spirit. Although poles apart, the two states have striking similarities. Each condition takes a person out of himself, removes the inhibitions, causes one to be more expressive and to more freely verbalize deep feelings. That's why the reserved, repressed Sirionos rarely used the intimate word.

The word "*nyesecua*" is still used by drunkards, but it is also now in the Siriono Scriptures. It is an expression of deep love only drunkards felt free enough to use until these Indians were transformed by the Spirit of love.[206]

When Eunice Pike was translating John 3:16 into the Mazatec language, she translated most of it without too much trouble, but she couldn't figure out how to render "should not perish" into Mazatec. In Spanish the phrase was "should not be lost" and Eunice told her language assistant several hypothetical stories in an attempt to get her to express lostness in her language. However the assistant didn't catch on.

Finally Eunice said, "Your little niece Rosa left the house one afternoon and didn't come back. You looked for her and couldn't find her. It got dark and you didn't know where Rosa was. What did you say? Rosa is . . ."

The assistant blurted out, "Rosa is sleeping someplace else."

Still no success, so Eunice moved on to other verses, hoping she'd eventually come across the right word. Then a couple weeks later her assistant picked up a fountain pen and drew a line on her arm. Eunice took the pen and wrote the girl's name on her hand.

"There now," Eunice said in broken Mazatec, "if you are lacking yourself, here is your name."

The girl chuckled and corrected her. "You mean if I am *lost*, here is my name."

Eunice had her word.

The last phrase of the verse, "shall have everlasting life," also posed a problem. Eunice thought maybe the word for "heart" was synonymous with "life." She tried it in another verse, "We know that

---

206 Ibid., 158–59.

we have passed from death to life, because we love our brothers" (1 John 3:14). When she said this in Mazatec to the language assistant, the girl asked, "Are you saying, 'We know that when we passed by [life], we died of heart disease?'"

No matter what Eunice tried, she couldn't discover how to say, "shall have everlasting life." Finally someone murmured that they wouldn't say, "has everlasting life." They'd say, "shall have not-death." So for a while the translation read: "Whoever believes in him shall have not-death."

Then one day when referring to life, a Mazatec woman said *"kjoavijnachon"* instead of "not-death." Eunice's partner couldn't believe it.

She asked the woman, "Do dead people have *kjoavijnachon*?"
"No."
"Do people who are living all have *kjoavijnachon*?"
"Yes."

The translators were finally able to render the last phrase of John 3:16 literally.[207]

Other literal renditions of John 3:16 read thus:

Yagua: "God loved those living on earth so that he sent his only Son, so that if anyone will believe [as a regular practice] on him, his soul won't get irretrievably lost; he will then [with implication of rather] forever be always for keeps with him."

Iquito: "God loved-long-ago-continually-it-is-said muchly people. Therefore he sent-long-ago-it-is-said his-Son people to. A person believing-obeying him, he forever will-live-into-the-indefinite-future-it-is-said. Not he will die."

Orejon: "God very much loving those who live here on earth gave the only Son he had. Those believing him will not be lost. They will never stop living."

Cocama: "Like that, very much God loved those-on-our-world, therefore, he gave his Son to them. Just one was his Son, the one from him. He gave he who was God's heart him [his Son] that they might have life, all those who are his believers, that they might not be lost."

---

207 Pike, *Not Alone*, 64–67.

Burera: "The First One—he stomach-laughed toward us men and women. With his nose he stomach-laughed toward us. His Son he gave to us—the only one. He gave him to us so that anybody his belief he elevates toward him, never does he die go-forever; but he will go on living."[208]

Of course, in explaining the gospel, translators must present Christ as the mediator between sinful humanity and holy God. In the former days before the gospel transformed lives, the Kanites of Papua New Guinea frequently fought murderous battles between villages. A battle was only stopped when a strong leader would stand between opposing forces and call for them to lay down their spears. One side would bring sugar cane and the other, *tanget* (victory leaf shrub). A crossed line called *yofa* would be made between the two groups, and an era of peace would begin.

As Joy McCarthy and Gwen Gibson translated the New Testament into Kanite, the tribe learned that Jesus is the Strong Man who stands in the middle between God and sinners, making peace by the blood of his cross. Knowing this, the term *yofa yosa* (crossed tree) took on profound spiritual meaning to the Kanites.[209]

A reading of Hebrews 9:12 in the Wantoat language of New Guinea illustrates how translators must translate the source of peace into concepts the receptor people can readily understand:

> Christ entered part of the forbidden [holy] house and then went into the most forbidden house [holy of holies]. And wanting to give God something very good [an offering], he did not take sheep's blood or little [cow's] blood when he entered. He died for us and his blood came out. Taking that, he entered. And in order that God will not strike us for our sins he gave that very good thing to God. And so it will always be that God will feel cool [peace] toward us.[210]

When Ernest and Marjorie Richert were translating Ephesians 2:14 into the Mid-Waria language of Papua New Guinea, they found

---

208 Hefley, *Searchlight on Bible Words*, 136–38.
209 Ibid., 48.
210 Ibid., 57–58.

that a literal rendering of the phrase, "He himself [Christ] is our peace," held no meaning to the tribespeople.

The Richerts explained to their translation assistant that by Christ's death he had made possible a reconciliation between God and humanity. The assistant suggested they use the term *"soota"* in place of the word "peace."

The *soota* is a twelve-inch wing feather of the white cockatoo. The feather is the peace symbol of the Mid-Warias. The peace-king carefully split the feather in an intricate herringbone design all the way down to the hollow quill. At the appropriate time the peace-king would appear at the scene of battle wearing the *soota* feather in his hair. Immediately the fighting would stop, and the warring groups would come together to celebrate a feast marking a new period of tranquility. When the Mid-Warias read, "He is our *soota*," they understood what Christ did.[211]

---

211 Ibid., 61.

CHAPTER NINE

# Kingdom Talk

AMONG THE PROMINENT THREADS EXTENDING throughout the Bible is the subject of the kingdom of God. God, the King of kings, has always had a people. To the English reader the concept of kingdom/nation suggests an area or a people ruled by a king or president. Biblically, God's kingdom is a people or a person under the sovereign rule of God.

We may have experienced the *freedoms* associated with being part of a "kingdom," but in some cultures their only experience of "kingdom" has connotations of *ruthlessness, favoritism,* or *crass exploitation*. And in Western nations we often emphasize *quantity*, while many cultures focus on *quality*. We emphasize *product* and *productiveness*; some cultures embrace the *process*. We Christians emphasize *eternal* life; some cultures cherish all the fullness of the *present* moment (a few don't even have a future tense). Thus, from the outset it is crucial for translators to realize that many cultures view kingdom life differently than the Western mind.

Bible translators frequently have difficulty even finding a word for "kingdom." In fact, one missionary in Central Africa thought he'd been telling people to "enter the kingdom of heaven," when actually he'd been saying, "Go sit on a stick."[212]

Roy and Georgialee Mayfield discovered that the Central Cagayan Agta Negritos of the Philippines have nothing in their culture about kings and kingdoms—in fact, they don't even have tribal or village leaders. Any vague ideas of leadership are limited to the male head in a family.

Finally Roy's language assistant thought of a word that means "an area which one defends or protects." Contrary to Anglo tradition, which concentrates the idea of kingdom upon the leader, Agtas focused upon the sacred responsibility of the leader to defend and protect his subjects. Thus, the word would roughly correspond with our word, "protectorate." So the Mayfields translated a verse such as John 3:3: "If a man is not born again he cannot have any part or share in God's protectorate."[213]

In many cultures, the biblical teaching of mutual servanthood is much more easily understood than Paul's teaching of striving to win a race. Among these peoples, community solidarity and harmony is valued far above competition and individual achievement. In fact, in some Central African cultures, if an individual stands out in the crowd by consistently competing to win or dominate others, he or she could well be suspected of practicing sorcery to achieve such victories.[214]

In the Tangoan language of the New Hebrides the idea of kingdom has a rich cultural background. A chief over a number of villages marks his kingdom in a distinctive way. He places leaves from a particular type of tree beside the trails along the outer boundaries. He considers himself seriously responsible for maintaining peace and protecting people within this area. Strangers entering and seeing the leaf know they are answerable to him for their conduct. Such an area is known as the "peace of Chief ————." So the translator expressed the concept of God's kingdom: "*Tamata noni Moli Koti*" (the peace [kingdom] of the Lord [Chief] God).[215]

---

212 Nida, *God's Word*, 16.
213 Hefley, *Searchlight on Bible Words*, 154–55.
214 Wendland, *The Cultural Factor*, 123.
215 Hefley, *Searchlight on Bible Words*, 154.

Translators were also wondering how to render the term "God's kingdom" in Apache. An Apache assistant suggested that when a tribal chairman is in authority over an area, the Apaches say that the area is "in his hand." Thus, the kingdom of God became "those who are in God's hand."

In the Navajo language there are no words for king or kingdom. The word for headman is derived from a verb meaning, "to move the head from side to side," as in making an oration or influencing people by moving the head. This word could be used for "leader," but translators wondered how to say, "the highest ruler." Ultimately, the best they could do was the rather laborious, "of those who move the head from side to side, this one is the greatest."

A word for crown was even more remote. The Navajos have never even worn the elaborate headdress of some American Indians. The translator eventually rendered crown, "the hat of the one who moves his head from side to side."

The hat is key in the Nsoq culture, in which the kind of hat a man wears signifies his rank in the society. Also the location of a leader's chair within the Nsoq palace indicates his rank or importance. The great leaders subordinate to the king have chairs arranged to the left of the throne in order of importance. If someone were to claim a chair on the right, he would be claiming superiority to the king.

This presented a problem in the translation of Acts 2:34,35 where a quotation is drawn from the Old Testament, where God the Father speaks to his Son, "The Lord said to my Lord: 'Sit at my right hand until I make your enemies a footstool for your feet.'"

To the Nsoq, this would mean God the Father was making his Son greater than himself. Karl Grebe, the translator, changed the phrase to, "Sit on my top chair until I make your enemies a footstool for your feet."

Similarly, in Mark 10:37, James and John ask that in Christ's kingdom one could sit on Christ's left, the other on Christ's right. This was reworded to read: "We want to sit on the two top chairs in your kingdom."[216]

---

216 Translation Treasures, *In Other Words*, January–February 1975, 6.

Often when we speak of the kingdom of God, we imply leadership—God's preeminence over human hearts through Christ. How do various cultures view leadership?

The Binumarien people follow an interesting custom in appointing someone to hold an important position in a village. At a village gathering the chief will point directly at a person to signify that he has been chosen by the village council. This person is then said to be "the one who has had a hand put on him." Thus, when translators Desmond and Jennifer Oatridge came to the powerful verse in which Peter declares, "You are the Christ, the Son of the living God" (Matt 16:16), they wondered how to translate it most effectively. A language assistant suggested that it could be best translated: "You are the One who from a long time before has had a hand put on him, the Son of the staying-alive God."

That night wives, children, and other clan members were called together, and the language assistant read them the verse. They were impressed and discussed Christ far into the night. Before this, the idea of Christ as Lord held no meaning to the Binumariens; now they were beginning to understand.[217]

A person's leadership is expressed uniquely among the Muinane Indians of the Amazon. A person of power or importance is termed "heavy." Of course, they don't mean this literally, any more than we do when we say a person is "throwing his weight around." Thus, in Acts 13:50 the Muinane language reads: "The Jews stirred up the heavy men and women of the city" against Paul.

Also, to be "heavy-mouthed" means to speak with power and authority. A Scripture such as Matthew 7:28,29 would read in Muinane: "When Jesus had finished saying these things, the crowds were amazed at his teachings, for he taught as a heavy-mouthed one and not as their teachers of the law."[218]

The kingdom authority principle is difficult to communicate in some cultures. In the loosely structured Lengua society of Paraguay there is no strong chieftainship, much less a concept of kings, kingdoms, or thrones. Thus, to say, as in Hebrews 1:8, "Your throne,

---

217 Hefley, *Searchlight on Bible Words*, 59.
218 Translation Treasures, *In Other Words*, July–August 1974.

O God, will last forever and ever," poses semantic difficulties. Therefore, translators decided to render the phrase: "You, God, are the chief unendingly."[219]

Even more difficult is the Bacairi culture of Brazil where they believe that every person should do as they please. No one can coerce or discourage anyone from doing anything. This practice extends to children as well. A few members of the society gain respect because of knowledge or age, but even the chief has no real authority over others. Translators must take great care as they communicate the biblical chain of command.[220]

When translating passages about Christian leadership, translators realized a particular Valiente Indian term may not be suitable. Those in authority are said to be "on the handle."[221] In other words, the ruler figuratively holds the hunting knife of leadership in his hand. Anyone who defies him can only grasp the blade and, therefore, be at great disadvantage. This seems to endorse a cutthroat (no pun intended) brand of leadership in place of the biblical model characterized by servanthood. Thus it must be communicated clearly that God has set us apart to be, not tyrants, but holy examples.

The Gospel of Mark was being translated into the Orejon language of Peru. There was a translation quandary when Dan and Virginia Velie reached the word "holy" in Mark 6:20. They did find a word which meant "chosen for a special purpose; dedicated for a specific use," but the word was used in reference to a witch doctor's pipe. The intimate association with the witch doctor did not seem appropriate when referring to John the Baptist's dedication to a spiritual purpose. With further inquiry, however, Dan learned that the word was also used in regard to a certain tree the Orejons carefully chose and nurtured to later use as a canoe. So he used this word accompanied by the word for "God" to imply "chosen for a godly purpose."[222]

With God as our King and Christ as our holy elder brother, we are each then appointed or set apart as leaders and priests under them. We must obey God's kingdom authority in our lives, and we become

---

219 Nida, *Language Structure and Translation*, 75.
220 Larson, *Meaning-based Translation*, 43.
221 Nida, *God's Word*, 19.
222 Hefley, *Searchlight on Bible Words*, 149.

servant leaders to others. If God is really sovereign in our lives, we will inevitably bear spiritual fruit, though it may legitimately differ in type and amount.

An old Filipino woman listened intently as translator Hazel Wrigglesworth related to her the parable of the sower from Luke 8. When Hazel said, "And other seed fell on good ground and sprang up and bare fruit . . . some a hundredfold," the woman wriggled her nose.

"This good hundredfold crop will not be clear to our Manobo people," she said. "Especially our old folk. We have a Manobo expression to describe a good crop. We like to say, 'You have only to pass the winnowing tray over the top of the ripened rice in order to fill it.'" If believers are truly growing good fruit, all God will have to do is pass his winnowing tray over our lives to see the fruit.[223]

The Burera language of the Aborigines is extremely literal. David and Kathleen Glasgow learned this quickly when they began translating. For example, they hit a snag when they tried translating Mark 4:20: "Others, like seed sown on good soil, hear the word, accept it, and produce a crop—thirty, sixty or even a hundred times what was sown."

The Bureras could understand hearing the word and accepting it, but their language could not adequately interpret people being compared to seeds in soil which produce a crop. Bureras think concretely, so they would envision actual pieces of fruit emerging all over people's bodies. The Glasgows had to translate the segment very simply: "They hear the word of God, they get it, then they become good."[224]

In some sense, each of us are leaders in someone's life, though leadership means something different biblically than it does in secular society. Being a leader involves being like salt to the people who pass through our lives. It is interesting to note some varied renditions of Christ's challenge that we be those who check the moral corruption in the world, so that it doesn't quickly degenerate in its own moral rottenness (Matt 5:13):

---

223 Ibid., 124.
224 Ibid.

Jur Modo: "Your role is to be like salt for the people of the earth. However when salt has finished and has leaked out . . . by what sort of means will it be made to return and be savory? It is no longer any use at all, but . . . just to be thrown away and trodden on by feet."[225]

The Message: "Let me tell you why you are here . . . to be salt-seasoning that brings out the God-flavors of this earth. If you lose your saltiness, how will people taste godliness? You've lost your usefulness and will end up in the garbage."[226]

Swahili (Union): "You are the salt of the world. But if the salt is harmed, what will be put in so that it may be seasoned? It isn't worth again at all but to be thrown outside and trampled on by people."[227]

English composite: "It is you who are the salt of the earth, but if the salt should lose its strength, what is there left to restore its saltiness? It is good for nothing anymore save being cast out and stamped under foot."

Whether we are salty preservatives of holiness in the world or those who spread God's "flavor" to those we meet, the individuals we touch symbolize spiritual victory and will someday constitute our crown in the kingdom.

Returning from a successful hunt, an Engenni man of Nigeria shouts, "*Ugo! Ugo!*" as he lifts a wild pig in triumph. This is the Engenni word for "eagle." The eagle and its feathers are used as a sign of victory. The whole town congratulates the man, and women break into dance.

After witnessing this scene, translators Elaine Thomas and Joy Clevenger returned to their work. They had reached the point in 1 Thessalonians in which Paul calls the Christians there his "crown" (Cf. 1 Thess 2:18). The Engenni have no word or concept for crown, but the translators had another idea. Why not bring in the idea portrayed by the triumphant hunter? So they translated Paul's expression: "You are the ones who make me shout 'Eagle!'"[228]

---

225 Andrew Persson, email message to author, May 5, 2002.
226 Eugene Peterson, *The Message: The Bible in Contemporary Language* (Colorado Springs, CO: NavPress, 1995).
227 Oliver Stegen, email message to author, May 6, 2002.
228 Translation Treasures, *In Other Words*, March 1975, 6.

Flowing out of our celebration of God's character and the supernatural things he does in us and through us to others, we practice the sacrifice of worship. Any discussion about worship must begin with the Holy Spirit. If it were completely up to us self-centered creatures, we would probably spend most of our time worshiping ourselves, with a few minutes set aside pretending to worship others in order to get our way.

An indispensable part of kingdom life involves offering all we are and have to God. Before we can be filled with the Spirit in this way, we must recognize how much we need him. The Kare language of Central African Republic pictures the Holy Spirit as "the One who falls down beside you." That is, one who accompanies, protects, and sustains us on our pilgrimage, much as in Kare country, where a helper accompanies the traveler through hard and dangerous bush.

Jim and Judy Butler were struggling to translate the idea of people being filled with the Spirit into the Tzutujil language of Guatemala. One could not say in Tzutujil that people were filled with something. Even stating that "their hearts were filled with the Holy Spirit" wasn't grammatically appropriate. Though the Butlers' final construction was still weak, they finally settled on "with all their heart they were guided by the Holy Spirit."

Almost two years later, Jim Butler happened to read a phrase in Tzutujil: "The canoe was filled in with people." He changed the verse to read: "The Holy Spirit filled [intransitive verb] in their hearts." When Butler asked his assistant, the man confirmed that this adequately expressed that the Holy Spirit was in them completely.[229]

In both the Tonga and Chewa languages the word "worship" has many facets and must be contextually specified as either "pray," "ask," "beg," "thank," "sacrifice," "honor," or the like.[230] For example, at the Areopagus Paul started out with: "Men of Athens, I see that in every way you are very religious" (Acts 17:22) ( . . . you are big worshipers or god-honorers).

In Folopa there is no word for the concept of religion; at least not one neat, little term. Though the Folopas' constant preoccupation

---

229 Ibid.
230 Wendland, *The Cultural Factor*, 71.

with the spirit world makes them very religious, they didn't see it as such. Finally, translator Neil Anderson had to render Paul's words: "I see that you are very much a praying-all-the-time people."

Paul continued, "For as I walked around and looked carefully at your objects of worship, I even found an altar with this inscription: To An Unknown God" (Acts 17:23).

The Folopa had no ideal term for "worship" either. The closest concept for worship was a word meaning "high regard for authority," literally "putting up as superior and dying under." The strength of the concept is the acknowledgement that everything God does is unquestionably superior. The weakness of the term is that it implies no appreciation or adoration. It was not the perfect word, but it was the best that could be found at that time.[231]

In contrast, for the Cuicatec Indians of Mexico, the word for worship may be a little light on reverence, but it's very high on adoration. It comes from the same root as that for a dog wagging its tail, implying the idea of worship as "wagging the tail before God." It is not the kind of idea we normally associate with worship in Western usage, and some might even consider the concept a bit sacrilegious. But for the Cuicatecs the phrase indicates unwavering loyalty and intimate devotion.[232] After all, isn't the dog a perfect example of such an attitude? Whenever a dog glimpses his master, he almost jumps out of his skin with excitement. His ears perk, his tail wags, and he stumbles all over himself just trying to please, trying to honor this being who feeds him, walks him, and occasionally gives him a doggie treat. That's worship.

---

231 Anderson, *In Search*, 202.
232 Sanneh, *Translating the Message*, 195.

CHAPTER TEN

# Heart, Liver, or Intestines?

It is interesting the way various cultures describe their inner person—sometimes they speak of emotions separately, other times their expressions encompass the soul or solely the thinking capacity. However, their expressions and some of the organs by which they refer to the inner person sound strange to us in the West.

In Conob, a Mayan language, the seat of the will and reason is considered the throat.[233] In the Tonga and Chitonga languages of Zambia, the seat of deepest emotions is the intestines. Thus a verse such as Matthew 15:32 could read in Tonga: "Jesus called to his disciples and said, 'My intestines are twisted with compassion for these people; they have been with me three days.'"[234]

Among the Anuak of Africa, to say one's "liver is bad" means a person is evil; "his liver is shallow" means a person is unsociable; "his liver is white" means a person is kind; "his liver is burned" means a person is irritable; "his liver is cold" means a person will not impolitely begin eating ahead of others (many American kids must have warm livers).[235]

---

233 Nida, *Language Structure and Translation*, 44.
234 Wendland, *The Cultural Factor*, 128–29.
235 Larson, *Meaning-based Translation*, 115.

In some languages such as Uduk, the liver represents the emotions of a person's inner being, just as we English speakers describe them as being in our hearts. For example, where Jesus said, "Do not let your hearts be troubled" (John 14:1), the Uduks would substitute "liver" for "heart" and then add another interesting little twist. Thus it reads: "Do not shiver in your livers; you believe in God, believe also in me."[236]

At one point, a Urubu tribesman said, "My wife has sent her liver to her dogs." The translator indicated complete ignorance of his meaning. The tribesman explained that his wife was worried and preoccupied about her dogs, which she had left behind in the village. He continued, "My wife has also sent her liver to the bananas." She had recently transplanted a special variety of banana tree. Tribal legend said that if someone other than the owner eats the first bananas produced, the eater will become ill.

So, unintentionally, the translators had learned the Urubu expression for worry.

They now knew that segments from passages in Matthew 6 would be rendered: "Do not send your liver to what is going to happen tomorrow, do not send your liver to the food you will be eating or the clothing you will wear. Is not life more important than food and clothing?"[237]

Adversity is a universal obstacle for humans, and we sometimes give way to anxiety. Several English translations interpret Christ's words to the disciples during the storm in Mark 6 as, "Be of good cheer!" or "Take heart! Don't be afraid." But in the Waorani tongue, it is expressed, "Why ever, for goodness sake . . . do you all fear?" Implied in the expression is "Stop it now!" Among these people, in place of gentle sympathy, a stern rebuke or challenge from the heart is often expected when a fellow Waorani faces adversity.[238]

Millie Larson was translating the New Testament for the Aguarunas of northern Peru. She hit a snag when she came to Colossians 1:18 where Paul declares, "He [Christ] is the head of

---

236 Nida, *God's Word*, 23.
237 Hefley, *Searchlight on Bible Words*, 123.
238 Ibid., 172.

the body, the church." Of course, she realized that, since the brain is the controller of bodily impulses, Paul meant Christ is the one who directs or controls his body, the church. However, as far as the Aguarunas are concerned, the head does not control the body, it is the heart. In fact, their word for "think" is the word *"heart"* in verb form, so when they think, they "heart themselves" (literal translation). The head does not refer either to the intellect, will, or emotions.

Larson had two basic choices. She could translate the word as "head" and try to explain scientifically how and why the head controls the human body; however, that could bog the reader down with bulky description. She decided to adapt the text to the understanding of the Aguarunas and communicate that Christ is the "heart." Larson translated the verse: "All those sold to him, they are like one body and its true heart is Christ."[239]

Rincon is a dialect spoken by the Zapotec people of Mexico. When translators came to Luke 24:32, "Were not our hearts burning within us?" a correct translation required the opposite concept. The new translation read, "Did not our hearts *cool* within us?" In Rincon, a burning heart indicates anger, while a cool heart reflects what the passage intended—a deep interest and pleasure.[240]

The Aboriginal languages are somewhat similar in this regard. When Aborigines hear an ordinary story, they stay hot as always; but when they hear a story that moves or affects them, it makes them "cold."[241]

Sometimes in English we speak of someone living in sin as having a "black heart." For Chewas, a black heart means something very different. For instance, in Job 33:20, describing sickness and depression, Elihu speaks of someone whose "soul loathes the choicest meal." In the Chewa language this is rendered, "Food makes his heart black."[242]

Contrary to our expression, having "a big heart" in Shilluk of the Sudan is used of the miserly, while its opposite is used for those seen as generous. The Sudanese picture the miserly as those who selfishly

---

[239] Ibid., 50.
[240] Ibid., 13.
[241] Ibid., 138.
[242] Wendland, *The Cultural Factor*, 131.

store things in the heart, making the heart oversized. Generous persons, by contrast, acquire a small heart by giving away what they have to others.[243] In still another culture, to love is to "hide another in one's heart."[244]

For the desert-dwelling Guajiro Indians of South America, there are many common expressions about the heart which reflect thought and emotion. To have a "hard heart" means one is able to endure trials. A "good heart" means contentment, and a "bad heart" means sadness. A person with a "powerful heart" is one who despises others. If someone says, "I do not have two hearts," this person thinks she's dying. If she adds that her "heart is small," she is at the point of death.[245]

In English the expression "hard-hearted person" is derogatory, denoting a person who is stubborn, cold, uncaring. However some languages don't use this expression. In the Shipibo language of Peru, an uncaring person is known as a person whose "ears have no holes," meaning supposedly that he closes his ears to the needs of others.[246]

Also, a hard heart isn't negative in every language. Early in the translation process with Guatemala's Ixil Indians, Ray Elliott reached Mark 16:14 with his language assistants. When Jesus used the term "hardness of heart" (KJV) for the eleven disciples, he meant their cold reluctance to believe he had risen. However, if an Ixil Indian calls someone hard-hearted, it is a high compliment. It means a person has great toughness and courage. In discussion with Ixil helpers, it became obvious that the constantly barefooted Indians definitely knew the meaning of rock-hard foot callouses, so Elliott decided to translate the verse portion: "Jesus scolded them because they did not believe and because their hearts had callouses."[247]

As in the Ixil dialect, to the Fulani "to harden the heart" means literally to show bravery. In Fulani, the English idiom "hardening the heart" is expressed by the phrase "hardening the head."[248] And

---

243 Sanneh, *Translating the Message*, 196.
244 Nida and Reyburn, *Meaning across Cultures*, 41.
245 Translation Treasures, *In Other Words*, March 1976, 6.
246 Eugene Nida and Charles Taber, *The Theory and Practice of Translation* (Leiden, Netherlands: Brill, 1969), 106.
247 Hefley, *Searchlight on Bible Words*, 142.
248 Nida and Waard, *One Language to Another*, 34.

in several African languages a "hard-hearted" person is said to have ears that are hard or a hardened stomach.[249]

Mark 3:5 is another Scripture in which hardness of heart is mentioned. When Rachel Saint came to this verse, her Waorani helpers quickly equated hardness of heart with "hearts like a jungle." Thus, to them Jesus was angry about the "jungle-hearts" of the Pharisees. To the Waoranis, jungle also means dense, uninhabited land. Saint pointed out that, figuratively, that's how the Waoranis saw the hearts of the Pharisees."[250]

Harold and Diana Green translated the Scriptures into Palikur, an Indian dialect of equatorial Brazil. They learned some rather interesting ways the Palikurs used physical references to reflect their emotional state. The Indians considered their middle or their abdomen as the center of emotional and intellectual activity. Some of their expressions were:

"My abdomen is cold" (My heart is at peace).
"My abdomen is swollen" (I am furious).
"My abdomen hurts for him" (I am sorry for him).
"His abdomen is straight" (His heart is true).
"My abdomen is dripping" (I am very frightened).
"His abdomen is broken" (He is dead).
"I like my abdomen" (I am happy).

The Mixtec Indians of Mexico also have some unusual ways of describing inner emotions. To forgive is to "open big inside." To forget is to "get lost inside." To be disdainful is to "dry up inside." To love is to "be poor inside." To wonder or be amazed is to "sink from view inside." And to be undecided is to "be two inside." It would be interesting to know why "being poor inside" represents love to these people or how "drying up inside" represents disdain.[251]

No matter how different peoples express issues of the mind and heart, God understands and reaches out to the most remote language groups to win their hearts to his everlasting truth.

---

249 Beekman and Callow, *Translating the Word of God*, 147.
250 Hefley, *Searchlight on Bible Words*, 143.
251 Ibid., 181.

# CHAPTER ELEVEN

# Being Strong on God

CHRISTIANITY IS ALL ABOUT TRUST IN A GOD who cannot lie. Faith must be exercised in Christian conversion, and it must grow increasingly in daily experience. This means believing in God's wisdom and power to the point in which we are completely at rest in his protective palm. In one African language this epitome of wisdom is pictured as an "old one with a single hair."[252] Perhaps the word picture is of an elder so ancient and wise that he has only one hair left.

"Believe" is often one of the most difficult biblical words for missionaries to identify in other languages. Hazel Spotts, translator for the Mazahua language in Mexico, usually used the Mazahua word *nejme*, which implies not only faith but obedience. When she reached Romans 4, where it speaks of Abraham's faith being counted as righteousness, she knew the word *nejme* would not be appropriate. The language helper affirmed that this implied it was both Abraham's belief and his good works that counted as righteousness. Finally Spotts recalled a word which meant literally "to plant in the heart." The use of this word expressed accurately that Abraham was counted as righteous because he had planted God in his heart.[253]

---

252 Nida and Taber, *Theory and Practice*, 106.
253 Hefley, *Searchlight on Bible Words*, 21.

The gospel was being translated into the Jur Modo language of southern Sudan. Translator Andrew Persson noticed that the Jur Modos were adopting a very generic word for "have faith/believe." The word *meri* meant "to think about." The word intersected vaguely with the idea of belief but certainly didn't carry much of the meaning of the Greek word *pistis*. Even worse, the word had secondary uses such as "worry about" or "be sad about." Consequently, people would be urged to *meri* in Jesus, then they would sing a hymn about how Jesus will remove our *meri*, or there will be no sickness, death, *meri*, etc., in heaven. Persson knew this had to be confusing to thinking Jur Modos.

Jur Modo leaders could not come up with a more accurate word for faith. Finally, Persson tried describing what he was looking for to a translation helper. He said, "If your best friend is traveling to the city and you give him all your savings so that he can buy you a radio, you have *faith* that he'll use that money for a radio and not for himself."

"Ah," said the assistant, "I would put my head behind his talk."

So after testing this idiom on others, Persson translated placing one's faith in Christ as "Put your head behind the talk of Jesus."[254]

As in many languages, the Suena language of Papua New Guinea sometimes uses more than one term or phrase for a concept expressed in English with only one word. One Suena word for "believe" meant "to take hold of"—that is, to believe in the existence of something. Another word meant "I understand and it rings true to me." A third word was a colorful idiom that meant literally "to tie the back of your neck to someone." The idea was complete dependence or reliance on someone else, even before seeing the outcome. For example, a Suena commented, "You call for an airplane to come for you, then you tie the back of your neck to the plane." Thus, translators expressed Acts 16:31: "Tie the back of your neck to the Lord Jesus Christ, and you shall be saved."[255]

The word "believe" was puzzling in Mazatec, because an absolute equivalent was lacking. The Mazatecs seemed to tangle the words

---

[254] Andrew Persson, email message to author, December 5, 2001.
[255] Hefley, *Searchlight on Bible Words*, 18.

"believe," "hear," and "obey." A mother might say, "Hear me!" to her child when an English-speaking mother would say, "Obey me." When a Mazatec child was slow to obey, the mother might say, "Do you not believe?" It is true that the biblical "believe in me" implies not only belief but commitment. However, it was still difficult to select exactly the correct Mazatec word.[256]

For a long time, translator Lorrie Anderson could only find one word for "believe" in the Candoshi language of Peru. It was the word that means simply "to say it is true." In time, Anderson was surprised to learn there were at least seven different words in Candoshi for "believe." One word for trust meant "to love." A second word meant "to both hear and obey." A third term meant "to possess or hold as one's own." A fourth expression meant literally "to repeat after" and implied the carrying out of orders. A fifth word meant "to come to understand." But the word Anderson liked best of all was the word *tatomaama*: "to rest the whole weight completely upon." The word was used rarely because there are few humans upon which one can totally rely. Anderson used this word in verses that challenge readers to trust fully in the Lord.[257]

When translating into the Paez language of Colombia, Marianna Slocum realized that the only words for "faith" or "believe" were borrowed Spanish words which carried little meaning for the Indians. She sought help from her Paez translation helper to coin new idioms for "faith" in his language. The most common way the helper began expressing "faith" was by using the verbs "say" or "think." For example, in Mark 9:23 Jesus says, "Everything is possible for him who believes." In Paez it read: "If you just think, 'It is possible,' it will be possible with me." Another Paez word combination for "faith" became "ability-to-do-it." Thus, in Mark 5:36 Christ's exhortation reads: "Do not fear. Just remember my ability-to-do-it."[258]

Robin and Marva Farnsworth searched long and hard for ways to express "faith" or "belief" in the Manambu language of Papua New

---

256 Ibid., 23.
257 Ibid., 19–20.
258 Ibid., 25–26.

Guinea. They found the basic word *wuk*, which had a variety of uses including "to hear, know, feel, or obey."

Then one of the translation assistants used the word *wukijubir*, a word meaning "to firmly think or know something." The suffix "*-jibir*" could be added to many verb stems to indicate intensity and preparation for something. For example, a hunter would "look-*jibir*" when he steadily aimed at something before spearing it. An aged person would "do-*jibir*" because, recognizing he would soon die, he wanted all his affairs to be in order.

This concept seemed especially ideal for use in Scriptures such as John 14:1 where Jesus says, "Do not let your hearts be troubled; *wukijibir* in God, *wukijibir* also in me . . . I go to prepare a place for you." Here the belief as well as the intense anticipation of Christ's return is clearly expressed.[259]

Reginalda, a Chatino Indian, was extremely ill. Translator Kitty Pride did give her some medication, but the woman continued to experience weakness and paroxysms of coughing. Every day, Pride came to Reginalda's house and sang Chatino hymns and prayed. During one visit, the woman told Pride she was afraid to die. She asked what God's Book said about life after death. Pride read verses about heaven already translated into Chatino.

"You say there is no more pain or sickness there?" asked Reginalda. "No more sadness and poverty, with not enough to eat?" Pride assured her it was true.

Reginalda wanted to hear the song entitled "The Two Roads." She said she wanted to walk the narrow road the lyrics described. Then she asked if Pride would sing the song of God about not being alone. Pride sang "No, Never Alone," and left the home soon after.

The next day when Pride was admitted into the house, she found two women relatives lovingly dressing the dead body of Reginalda. Reginalda's husband stepped up to Pride with tears. He said, "She didn't cry out or anything as she died. She said she had found the narrow trail leading to God's place, and she wasn't afraid at all because Jesus Christ was with her; and she wasn't alone."[260]

---

259 Translation Treasures, *In Other Words*, Summer 1978, 6.
260 Pride, *Bread Is Not Enough*, 137–38.

Of course, in Christianity the idea of faith begins with an acknowledgment of guilt for sin and a trust that through Christ's death we can be forgiven. In one of the first sins, Cain murdered Abel, and God declared that Abel's "blood cried out to me from the ground" (Gen 4:10). If Neil Anderson had translated the text literally, the Folopas would have been completely mystified. He had to figure out a more straightforward way of saying that Cain's sin was not hidden and would be punished. The demand for justice in the Folopa language literally means "payback." So Genesis 4:10,11 was rendered: "Now you must be paid back for what you have done. You killed your brother and his blood went into the ground. Now I am going to curse the ground for you because of what you have done."[261]

Payback, incidentally, is a very crucial concept in the Folopa culture. For every act of harm, whether intentional or accidental, there always has to be some form of compensation to even out the score. When the translator accidentally tore the shirt of a Folopa man, the village exploded into an uproar until the translator gave the man some money to make up for the tear. This was not just a nice habit, it was imperative in their culture. However, it was very rare for anyone to step in and compensate for the damage someone else had done. Therefore it was especially amazing to the Folopa to learn that Jesus had voluntarily become the payback for the sins they had personally committed against God. This seemed to move them in an especially profound sense.[262] As Folopas became Christians, their lives changed, and Communion services held among the Folopa became extremely meaningful occasions. With no grapes or bread as such, they used lemon juice and sweet potato. It's all they had, and it was enough.[263]

Tom Headland really took on a challenge when he decided to translate the Bible into the Casiguran Agta languages of the Philippines. One difficulty was that most actions could be said a few hundred different ways.

Headland couldn't figure out how to correctly render the action in John 3:3: "No one can see the kingdom of God unless he is born

---

261 Anderson, *In Search*, 64–65.
262 Ibid., 155.
263 Ibid., 156.

again." According to his language helper, his first attempt meant literally that "unless a person caused a child to be born, the child could not go to the sky." Headland's second attempt was off the mark too. This attempt meant that "unless a woman bears at least two children she cannot go to the sky." He realized he was using the verb form "to give birth" instead of "to be born." But when the Dumagat language helper realized Jesus was actually saying an adult must be born again, he laughed heartily and declared how impossible this was. But later he approached Headland alone—perplexed, almost pleading, "What does that mean?" It was almost the same question Nicodemus had asked many centuries earlier.[264]

Receiving Jesus is another way of expressing being born again. Henrietta Andrews, translator of the Otomi dialect, had difficulty finding the simple word "receive" to use in John 1:12, "Yet to all who received him, to those who believed in his name, he gave the right to become children of God." Andrews kept finding specific words meaning "receive," but no general ones. In other words, there was a word that meant "to receive a small object like a coin or egg into one's hand." There were others for grasping with both hands, holding a child or a large object, etc. Finally she came across a word that she thought would fit. It was used in the expression "to take or receive a wife," but it was also used to mean "to take into one's home [or life] to stay permanently."[265]

Explaining salvation in the Chamula language of Mexico would literally sound something like this:

> If nothing you do has any flavor (enjoyment) but offers only bitterness, only God can make you fat (healthy, robust) inside. If what is under your hands and feet (under your control) is not turning out right . . . if you do not see people well (care deeply from the heart) from the inside of your heart, you must come to Jesus Christ with a straight heart (earnestly, honestly). Because Jesus has died for you, you can be well-off by him (receive his love and grace). If you ask him for forgiveness and

---

[264] Hefley, *Searchlight on Bible Words*, 166–67.
[265] Ibid., 173.

new life, he will save you. You will then be seen well (fully accepted) by the Lord.[266]

In a region of West Africa the word for "save" literally meant "to free," in the sense of granting relief from physical labor. Thus, children who attended missionary schools decided that their state of "salvation" meant the right not to do any work on roads or pay any tax. Salvation had no spiritual significance to them; they thought it symbolized political or economic freedom, and this fallacy had to be clarified. This smacks somewhat of the attitudes of the Thessalonians, whom Paul rebuked for imagining that Christ's expected return meant they could loll the days away in idleness.[267]

This biblical expression, "to be saved," is one that stirs the curiosity of those reading the Bible for the first time. When John Lind was translating Luke for the Sierra Popoluca Indians, an Indian came to the term *taciacputpa*, "to be saved."

"What does this word really mean?" he asked John.

John decided to answer with a question of his own. "How do you use that word?"

The Popoluca gave an example. "If a man were in jail for a crime he had committed and another man paid money to the proper authorities for the prisoner's release, this would be *taciacputpa*."

Lind went on to explain that this is essentially what Jesus did for humanity—humans were prisoners of sin and bound for an eternal sentence. However, Jesus came and paid our debt and saved us by dying in our place. The Indian verified that Lind was definitely using the correct expression for "to be saved."[268]

Joanne Shetler was searching for the corresponding Balangao term for "save" in John 3:17. She kept giving her language helper real-life illustrations, hoping to elicit a word meaning to "rescue, deliver, save, preserve from danger or death." The only word the helper could come up with meant "to get," and this seemed too weak.

Then she described a hypothetical Balangao scene in which a tribal lawbreaker is brought before a council to be judged and fined for

---

266 Hugh Steven, *They Dared to Be Different* (Irvine, CA: Harvest House, 1976).
267 Nida, *God's Word*, 47–48.
268 Hefley, *Searchlight on Bible Words*, 174.

the offense. An advocate or lawyer speaks on behalf of the accused and succeeds in winning the man's release. "What did the advocate accomplish for the accused?" asked Shetler.

The Balangao man replied, "He made him stand."

So she translated John 3:17, "God did not send his Son to sentence people to punishment but rather to make them stand."[269]

Rachel Saint had a terrible time discovering the expression for "to be saved" in the Waorani language. She listened, waited, asked, and prayed, but the only kind of rescues she heard about were descriptions of *how* people were rescued from very particular dilemmas.

One day Rachel described to some Waoranis every type of rescue she'd ever heard about. She recounted how little Bibanca had been rescued too late from the boa, how Aepi and Gomoki had been rescued from the river by Cyaento, how Nimo was rescued from the fire when, demon-possessed, she fell in. Rachel added an additional few hypotheticals, then asked, "How would you describe all these cases?" Finally she got the form for which she'd been searching: *aena beaenque*, or "He rescued us just for the sake of rescuing us!" This pictured perfectly the grace of God.[270]

In the Rincon dialect of Zapotec, one who "makes his heart walk to someone" is showing favor or grace toward that person. One who "goes in one's heart" to the Lord is reflecting faith. Thus Ephesians 2:8, "For it is by grace you have been saved, through faith," is translated, "Because God made his heart walk to you, he saved you. He saved you because you went to him in your hearts."[271]

A picture of grace in the Amahuaca language is the idea of loosing someone. Thus Ephesians 2:8 reads, "When you believe, God looses you, he looses you without paying. Not anything you have done or are doing. It is God's gift, it is not man's work."[272]

While translating for the Mazateco people, translators searched for a word for "wash," as in Christ washing our sins away. They first tried the word *tsacanejon*. However, they learned this meant merely washing the surface of something. It communicated the idea to the

---

269 Shetler, *And the Word Came*.
270 Hefley, *Searchlight on Bible Words*, 176.
271 Ibid., 138.
272 Ibid., 35.

Mazateco that Christ washed the bodies of believers. After further study, they substituted the suffix "*-ya*" (the inside) for "*-jon*". Using *tsacaneya* for "wash," the phrase read, "Christ washed us on the inside from our sins."[273]

The Amahuacas have a word for "forgiveness" which means "smoothing over dirt when drawings or marks have been made in it." In more modern Amahuaca use, it could also mean "wiping off dust where marks have been made," such as in the erasing of a chalkboard. The word fits exactly with the biblical promise that God wipes away the sins of those who trust in Christ.[274]

After we experience conversion, there is the growing trust that takes place with gradual spiritual maturity. All languages have ways to express that steady, mellowing trust that develops within us.

In the Piro language in eastern Peru, the most common word for "believe" is limited, and its meaning is quite shallow; it means no more than admitting that something did or did not occur. The best term for expressing daily trust in Christ is a compound word that means both "believe" and "obey". This reflects the personal involvement inherent in sanctifying faith.[275]

The Balangaos realized from the start that their faith had to involve obedience. In their words, it was called "facing God"—watching his eyes, watching how he does things, then reflecting his character by what you detect.[276] It is not unlike the process the Apostle Paul describes when he speaks of our unveiled faces reflecting God's glory as we're transformed from one degree of glory to another. Translator Joanne Shetler knew just how radical this transformation was when the Balangaos met peacefully with their mortal enemies, the Ifugaos.

Jim Loriot translated the New Testament into the Shipibo language. In this language, to have faith in God is best expressed (literally), "to be strong on God." To the Shipibo, this means that there is no strength at all without God and that we are strong only

---

273 Translation Treasures, *In Other Words*, April–June 1972, 15.
274 Hefley, *Searchlight on Bible Words*, 20.
275 Ibid.
276 Shetler, *And the Word Came*, 112.

when we rely completely upon him.[277] In the Aztec dialect, faith is defined as "following close after," and the Valiente Indians speak of faith with a hunting term meaning literally "catching God in the mind."[278]

The Balinese cannot say "believe in a person" per se. They express trust with the phrase: "to believe in the mouth of someone." This carries the idea of trusting in the words and character of an individual.[279]

In the Tzeltal language, "faith" may be rendered as "hanging onto God with the heart," and the peace that results is expressed in more than one African language as "sitting down in the heart," implying the true serenity of the Christian at rest.[280]

However, this is not to say that placing our full trust in Christ means that we can let down our guard and drift with the tide. We must gain discernment to distinguish between what is false and what is true, what is of God and what is not.

The Tagabili people of the Philippines weave baskets out of a type of bamboo. So much of life revolves around the basket weaving that cultural idioms have evolved from the trade. For example, the word for "defective bamboo" is also used in a proverb meaning, "There is no truth, no value in this. Do not believe it." Conversely, a reverse use of the "bamboo" word yields the expression, "This is not that which is to be discarded." Translator Vivian Forsberg used the expression in 1 Timothy 1:15: "This is the truth, this is not to be discarded. Believe it."[281]

In trying days, believers in every culture must be fortified, remain alert, and be "armed and ready" as we wait for Christ's return. Paul speaks of this personal fortification in 1 Thessalonians 5:8,9 where he challenges believers to put on the "breastplate" of faith and love and the "helmet" of salvation's hope. Faith, hope, and love can be quite abstract, and in many cultures, bodily protectors such as breastplates are completely unknown. However, the Samo tribe, for

---

277 Hefley, *Searchlight on Bible Words*, 20.
278 Nida, *God's Word*, 120.
279 Ibid., 126.
280 Hefley, *Searchlight on Bible Words*, 187.
281 Nida and Taber, *Theory and Practice*, 106.

example, utilizes a longhouse as both a home and a fortress. Each night logs are stacked to seal off the main entrance, and a watch is set. The watchman or *ayo* inspires community members, and the logs provide security against attack.[282] Thus, verse 8b might read in Samo: "Let us encourage ourselves with faith and love as our *ayo*, and our hope of salvation as the stacked logs of a longhouse." There is no greater reassurance.

---

282 Kraft, *Christianity in Culture*.

# CHAPTER TWELVE

# Hold the Ear and Give a Good Stomach

This chapter is about forgiveness but, much more fundamentally, it is about love. Without God's love within, God's brand of forgiveness is totally absurd. God instructs us to love even when we're having a terrible day, when we're disabled by illness or injury, when problems pile up with no solutions in sight, when a person has greatly wronged us—we are to love no matter what, and only Christ can make that possible.

The concept of love is not always an easy one to identify in a language. It took Dudley Peck and his wife ten years to discover the correct word for "love" in the Mam language (among the Mayans).[283] And in the Samo language, there is no word at all for "love." The Samo language and way of thinking is so concrete that love is not so much expressed as *demonstrated* by caring, encouraging, sharing, and disciplining as necessary.[284]

Though God's love is shown most powerfully in his forgiveness, the evangelist Bakht Singh of India doesn't try to convince his hearers

---

283 Coke, *Translation among the Maya*, 275.
284 D. Shaw, *Transculturation*. 195.

that God loves them. His goal is to illustrate this unique brand of love by offering God's forgiveness through Christ. This is clearly evident in this conversation with the man:

"Do you first preach to them about the love of God?"

Bakht Singh: "No, the Indian mind is so polluted that if you talk to them about love they think mainly of sex."

"Do you talk to them of the wrath of God?"

Bakht Singh: "No, they are used to that. All the gods are mad anyway. It makes no difference to them if there is one more who is angry."

"Do you preach only on the crucified Christ?"

Bakht Singh: "No, they would think of him as a poor martyr who helplessly died."

"Then what is your emphasis? Eternal life?"

Bakht Singh: "Not so. If you talk about eternal life the Indian thinks of transmigration. He wants to get away from it."

"What then is your message?"

Bakht Singh: "I have never yet failed to get a hearing if I talk to them about the forgiveness of sins and peace and rest . . . soon they ask me how they can get it, and then I can lead them to the *Savior* who alone can meet their deepest longings."[285]

In his translation work, when Perry Priest reached 1 John 4:11, "Beloved, if God so loved us, we also ought to love one another" (NASB), his Siriono language helper said, "Oh, the Siriono will never do that."

Priest agreed, "Not by yourselves you can't." Then he added with a grin, "God is the One who causes us to love each other."

"We Siriono say, 'That's just the way we are,'" said the assistant, "and we keep right on fussing, fighting, and ignoring God's Word. Even if God helps us, it is not probable that we will ever love each other."

A few weeks later the two were still deliberating over what Siriono word to use for "beloved." The most appropriate word seemed to be

---

285 G. W. Peters, "Is Missions Homesteading or Moving?" *Mennonite Herald* (1977): 21.

*sechesecua*, which means "the one I'm very fond of." However, the word was not used much except among close relatives.

Priest wasn't sure they should use this word. But his helper, Echobe, thought for a while, then said, "Use it. We should all say '*sechesecua*' to each other now that we are Jesus' friends."[286]

When Jesus said, "Love your enemies," in Luke 6:27,35, the natural word to use for "enemy" in the Iduna language of Papua New Guinea appeared to be *nibaina*. For many decades the Iduna forefathers had engaged in interclan fighting. During that period, one's enemies were often killed and eaten.

But when translators asked today's Idunas who they considered their *nibaina*, they only stared blankly in silence. Finally one tribesman spoke up. He said that this type of enemy belonged to the "dark times," the old days of brutal war. The translators probed for other terms meaning "enemy" without much success. Finally someone told of a man who refused to eat with them, even avoiding any contact at all. He was bitter and angry—for him they used a new word to the translators: *talahagi*. In the Scripture the translators tried substituting *talahagi* for *nibaina*. The impact on the Idunas was striking. Jesus actually had something to say about the treatment of their enemy of the present.

One tribesman prayed, "Enter my brother's liver and mind and give sweet talk to him that he may throw away his enmity." Another prayed, "We cannot blot out enmity or forbid anger in ourselves, but all things are in your power; so come to us and help us."

They were taking the first vital step toward loving their enemies.[287]

The Arabelas of northeastern Peru seemed to exhibit little love and tenderness to one another. One evening a baby was born in their village, but when translators Rolland and Furne Rich showed up to view the infant, the tiny form lay gasping, abandoned on the cold ground. When they asked why, an Arabela said indifferently, "Oh, it isn't right. It's dying."

---

286 Hefley, *Searchlight on Bible Words*, 158.
287 Translation Treasures, *In Other Words*, June 1976, 6.

Furne Rich scooped up the baby. Rolland helped her cut the umbilical cord, and they carried the baby to their thatched house. All night they kept the child warm, blanketed in a box, but by morning he was dead. There was no grief evident, even among the child's parents, when they learned of the death.

In the days following this incident, Rolland tried to find out a word for the type of love a mother might have for her child. When he asked the chief, the man just gave him a blank stare.

Several days later, in conversation with the chief, Rolland said, "Suppose that a jaguar should attack a son. The father hears the child's screams and runs to his aid. At the risk of his own life, the father beats the jaguar with a stick and rescues his son. Why would a father do this?"

Finally the chief was able to give the Arabela word for "sacrificial love," which Rolland used in expressing God's love.[288]

Translator Ron Swick realized that even a simple-sounding verse such as Matthew 9:5 could easily cause confusion to people hearing it for the first time: "Which is easier: to say [to a paralytic], 'Your sins are forgiven,' or 'Get up and walk'?"

Swick did some further exegesis on the verse to help him translate it more clearly: "No one would lightly claim he had the power to forgive sins; but a person is even less likely to claim he has the power to heal people and say 'pick up your mat and walk' because if he were a fraud he would be exposed immediately. But I will prove I can do the one by doing the other."

The eventual translation of the verse read literally: "A man will lightly say to a paralyzed man, 'I forgive your sin,' but he will not lightly say to him, 'Pick up your mat and walk,' because if the sickness remains, it will give him big shame."[289] Swick correctly captured the point that Jesus did the physically supernatural to show he could do the spiritually supernatural wonder of forgiving.

There are many diverse ways of expressing forgiveness of an offense in different languages. The Timorese say "to wash away,"

---

288 Hefley, *Searchlight on Bible Words*, 168.
289 Ibid., 164.

the Kipsigis say "to heal the neck," the Kpelle say "to turn one's back on," and the Shilluk say "to spit on the ground for someone."[290]

Perhaps out of reverence, the Otomis of Mexico use two entirely different words for "forgive," depending on whether it is God doing the forgiving or a human. Thus, both words must be used in verses such as the one where Paul challenges us to forgive others just as God for Christ's sake has forgiven us.[291]

At first glance the translation of Matthew 18:21 into the Waffa language of Papua New Guinea seems a far cry from "How often shall my brother sin against me and I forgive him? Up to seven times?" (NASB). But translator Mary Stringer found that the Waffa language expresses things in unusual and unique ways. (1) "Friends" are "one-language people." (2) For the concept of sin, the Waffa use "bad thing," but when you sin against a *person*, you don't do "bad things," you do "bad work." (3) Emotions are often tied to the stomach. To be sorry is expressed as "the stomach is being heavy." To be upset: "the stomach is being cross." To be angry: "the stomach is being painful." To act out in anger: "the stomach is being sour." If "the stomach is good," it means one is happy or pleased. The idea of thinking is expressed "to hold the ear." Thus, to express the idea of forgiveness, Stringer tried, "Hold the ear and give a good stomach to them." (4) The Waffas express numbers by referring to their fingers and toes.

Thus, Stringer's final rendition of Matthew 18:21 read: "Peter came and said to Jesus: 'How many times shall my one-language people give bad work to me and I could not hold the ear about these things and give a good stomach to them? Shall I do it two and two and the fifth finger and from the new, two?"

Verse 22 had inherent problems too: "Jesus said to him, 'I do not say to you, up to seven times, but up to seventy times seven" (NASB). Did he mean we should count up to 490 times and then stop forgiving? To count up to twenty, a Waffa would say, "Two [the thumb and first finger] and two [the next two fingers] and the fifth finger. And from the new [hand] two and two and the fifth finger. From the foot

---

290 Nida and Waard, *One Language to Another*, 39.
291 Beekman and Callow, *Translating the Word of God*, 155.

two and two and the fifth toe and from the other [foot] two and two and the fifth toe." A more succinct way of saying twenty in Waffa is to say "one man completed." Still, this is not exactly an economical method of counting large numbers.

If you wanted to say 490, you would have to say twenty-four men completed and two hands from another man. For the Waffa to count this up literally, it would appear so fanciful as to overwhelm their minds. However, since in the passage the Lord is emphasizing continual forgiveness, not simply a forgiving a specific number of times, the translators decided to write: "Don't just forgive seven times only. Do not count and do it. Do it over and over."[292]

Some Zapotec Indians of Mexico speak the Rincon dialect. As Robert and Katherine Earl learned their language, they discovered that instead of saying "I forgive you" to someone, Indians say, "My face heals toward you." Robert and Katherine were not certain how this expression originated, unless it simply reflected that a face with an evil eye and hateful expression was changed or healed to reflect softness and friendship again. In any case, when Scripture spoke of forgiveness, the Earls translated it as "the face healing" toward someone else.[293]

A Wycliffe Bible translator was trying to learn how the Amahuaca Indians ask forgiveness. He said to his language helper, "Suppose I should kill your brother. How would I ask for your forgiveness?"

The Indian answered, "You would say, 'Speak to me.'" He explained that when a great wrong is done, the offender and the offended may not speak for years. But when the offender finally says, "Speak to me," he wants to be forgiven. This phrase is understood to mean, "Prove to me that we're on speaking terms again."[294]

When James and Kay Kakumasu were preparing the first draft of Mark's Gospel in the language of Urubu, they discovered what sounds like a very strange expression to us Westerners. When two Urubu tribesmen had a fight but then later reunited and forgave each other, people would say, "Their livers returned to each other."

---

292 Hefley, *Searchlight on Bible Words*, 119–20.
293 Ibid., 121.
294 Translation Treasures, *In Other Words*, October–December 1972, 10.

One day, however, the Kakumasus' language assistant admitted that "Mair's [a god] liver does not return to us." Mair was their cultural hero, and this meant that he was a god who does not forgive. It was a pleasure for the translator to explain that the true God is able to forgive because of Christ's death on the cross. This forgiveness of sin was rendered, "You have sinned, but God's liver returns to you."[295]

The Boras of Peru have no single word for "forgive." An expression that appears to reflect the idea of forgiveness is that of "being let off of charges owed." For example, when Boras go to the Peruvian judge downstream because of lawbreaking and they are forgiven, they say, "He left off what he would charge us."[296]

Perry Priest had reached 1 John in his translation of the New Testament into the Siriono language. As he and his Siriono helper, Humberto, worked one morning, Humberto complained that his finger hurt.

Priest sympathized with him briefly and continued the translation. He knew the Siriono Indians often complained about aches and pains. Several times during the next hour, Humberto kept mentioning the finger. Finally Perry asked, "How did it happen?"

"My wife and I had a fight this morning," he admitted, "and she bit my finger."

Perry saw that the finger was hardly injured. The two men began discussing verses in 1 John that describe loving one another. In the middle of the discussion, Humberto stood up and said he'd return shortly. A few minutes later, he returned and said, "Everything is all right now between us. I talked with Julia and we prayed together. Now we can continue our work."

The Siriono Christians were learning to forgive and to ask forgiveness.[297]

---

295 Hefley, *Searchlight on Bible Words*, 122–23.
296 Ibid., 122.
297 Ibid., 162–63.

CHAPTER THIRTEEN

# Satan, Evil Spirits, and Headless Turkeys

MISSIONARIES SOMETIMES FIND THAT, though native peoples may have no previous exposure to the Bible, they already believe in a Satan figure. In fact, the Chontals called Satan by the title "older brother," thinking that if they used his proper name, he might think he was being summoned.[298]

While working among the Wantoats, Don Davis was trying to decide how to translate the word "lion" as in 1 Peter 5:8: "Your enemy the devil prowls around like a roaring lion looking for someone to devour."

Davis realized that, though the Wantoat people had no concept of what a lion is, lions could be described to them at length and in detail. But was Peter interested in educating people about lions and their ways, or was he simply using an animal well-known in his own place and time which would illustrate something about Satan's ways?

Davis sought to exegete Peter's basic purpose. A lion roars and prowls, eventually trapping and devouring prey. Similarly, Satan

---

298 Larson, *Meaning-based Translation*, 116.

works to undo our faith and to cause us to sin, bringing about spiritual ruin. This simile does not focus on the roar, nor on the lion's particular carnivorous activities—as though Satan was a cannibal. The roaring and devouring are closely figurative and illustrative of insatiable destructiveness. The human body is not Satan's primary target, as is the lion's. Rather, as the enemy of our souls, Satan's activities are directed against our faith, our spiritual life—the inner person. This is Peter's focus.

Since the lion itself was not focal to Peter's statement, the next problem was to find an equivalent animal in the Wantoat forest. Davis thought of one animal called the *yakun* which is infamous for its incessant attacks on animals such as pigs, chickens, and dogs. The attack is vicious and usually fatal. Victims are terrorized when a *yakun* approaches, being virtually defenseless against its superior quickness. Davis struggled with the *yakun* option. This animal did not roar, nor was it from the cat family. However, these factors were not crucial, as Davis had borne out.

Davis wanted a translation that retained the dynamic quality of the original and remained faithful to the intended message of the author. The first New Testament readers would have undoubtedly recognized the verse instantly as an urgent appeal to be on guard constantly lest Satan should attack and destroy them. Why lose the Wantoat readers in the abyss of an illustration which mystifies when a *yakun* serves beautifully to illustrate Peter's point?

So 1 Peter 5:8 now reads in Wantoat: "As the *yakun* furiously works against animals, so Satan works furiously against you all so that you all will fall."[299]

Sometimes it seems as if God provides the solution to a translation dilemma almost at the moment it occurs. Roy Mayfield was translating John 8:44 where Jesus says of Satan, "He is a liar and the father of lies." The idea of a father of lies was not one which Mayfield thought the typical Agta Filipino would comprehend. It was an unusual figure of speech.

About that time, Mayfield's Agta assistant interrupted the conversation to scold his little daughter who was under the elevated house

---

299 Hefley, *Searchlight on Bible Words*, 177–78.

playing with her brother and the Mayfield's youngest son. Agtas often scold indirectly rather than directly, addressing the offender in the third person. What the assistant literally said was, "That one there alone is originating." When asked why he said this, the assistant explained that it was because his daughter was dominating all the play of the children and she was wrongly initiating everything.

Mayfield immediately connected this with the verse in John. He asked the informant if he thought the term "initiator" would be appropriate in describing Satan. Now the assistant got the point. "Satan is a liar and the initiator of lies" communicated the idea clearly and accurately.[300]

Many people groups throughout the world live in terror of evil spirits. When Eunice Pike told an Indian woman her baby was pretty, the woman recoiled, thinking Pike was giving the baby "the evil eye." In their minds, this meant that a baby becomes vulnerable to evil spirits. This fear is so great among such groups as the Chols and the Mazatecs of Mexico that they will declare a new baby ugly and add other negative adjectives in the hope that evil spirits won't want the baby.[301]

Even individual words are sometimes perceived as evil. References to horns in Revelation may often have an evil connotation in relation to the symbolic beasts, etc. But in other Scriptures such as Psalm 89:17,24, the horn symbolizes the positive idea of strength. In one Turkish language, though, the horn is *always* understood as a symbol of evil. Thus, even in Scripture references in which the horn is a positive thing, it must be replaced by the word "power" or "strength."[302]

Similarly in the Chewa language, the word for "horn" must be changed if it is used in a positive context. But when the Psalmist claims that all the horns of the wicked will be cut off (Ps 75:10), it would seem to fit the Chewa culture. In Chewa, the word for "sorcerer" means "person of the horn," and the sorcerer stores and applies potions that are kept in magical horns. However, in the same

---

300 Ibid., 160–61.
301 Larson, *Meaning-based Translation*, 116.
302 Peter Kirk, email message to author, December 3, 2001.

verse, when the Psalmist states, "But the horns of the righteous will be lifted up," the words must be changed to read perhaps, "But the strength of the righteous will be lifted up."[303]

Translators must be careful which term they use for the Holy Spirit. In some languages, to native speakers "Holy Spirit" has meant little more than "white ghost," because "holy" is equated with cleanness or whiteness and "spirit" is interpreted as a ghost. In one case, the results were even worse. The word for "holy" actually meant "that which makes taboo," and the basic word for "spirit" meant primarily "an evil or malicious spirit."[304]

Terms used for demonic spirits must also be selected wisely. In the Chewa language, at first translators thought that the term *mzimu woipa* (bad ancestral spirit) would be synonymous with demon. However, according to Chewas, though a *mzimu* may trouble a person, it will do so only for disrespect or impiety toward a relative, not because it is inherently evil. A demon's whole existence, on the other hand, is devoted to wicked ends.

Some believe there is a complex hierarchy of spirits whose primary goal is to sabotage the people in some area of daily life. The Tarahumara Indians live in remote canyons and on windy plateaus in northern Mexico's Sierra Madre mountain chain. When Kenneth Hilton tried to translate Psalm 23 into Tarahumara, he encountered a problem. They have always believed that evil spirits reside in still waters. In fact, they even explain the cause of tragedy at times by saying, "I stopped by the still waters." So when Kenneth came to verse two, "He leadeth me beside the still waters" (KJV), he knew the Tarahumaras would interpret God as an evil deity. Instead he used the term, "refreshing waters," which the people see as beneficial.[305]

The Chuj Indians of Guatemala commonly attribute many things, including natural phenomena, to the activity of Satan or of evil spirits. This occasionally has caused them to read into Scripture their own superstitions.

---

303 Wendland, *The Cultural Factor*, 90.
304 Ibid., 81.
305 Hefley, *Searchlight on Bible Words*, 141.

For example, Acts 4:31 reads, "The place where they were meeting was shaken." A Chuj gave the translator this explanation: "The devil shook the place. Then because the people were all frightened, God sent the Holy Spirit to them."

The translator had to clarify that the place was shaken by God, so that the Indians wouldn't automatically assume that Satan had done it.[306]

Particular Scriptures, such as Christ's healings, also had to be clarified for the Tzeltal Indians. Tzeltals have always called in a shaman or witch doctor to "touch" the pulse in order to divine who cast a curse of sickness upon a person. Jesus also sometimes touched people when he healed them. Translators Marianna Slocum and Florence Gerdel had to take special care in translating Christ's physical contact so as to not portray him as a glorified witch doctor. When Jesus healed the leper in Mark 1:41, the translators portrayed Jesus as touching the eyes, not the pulse. In another instance, they adapted Mark 10:13 to read, "They brought children for him to lay his hands on their heads." It was always essential in Tzeltal that the place of touch be defined.[307]

In the same vein, when Acts 8:9–24 was being drafted into the Ifugao language of the Philippines, truth had to be clarified. A language helper asked, "Why couldn't Simon buy the power of the Holy Spirit with money? We buy power from the witch doctor. Can't we buy power from God?"[308]

The Mazatecs were very afraid of demons, mountain gods, evil eyes, and witchcraft. However, a translator noticed that when a girl named Filipa read in the Scriptures about unclean spirits she acted almost bored. It seemed as if she should have been excited about a Christ who could help people oppressed by unclean spirits.

One day the translator heard a mature Mazatec Christian pray that the Lord would protect them from "the good wind." What did the wind symbolize, and why ask protection against something good?

---

306 Ibid., 164.
307 Ibid., 143.
308 Beekman and Callow, *Translating the Word of God*, 161.

The translator recalled that the Indians made mat walls surrounding a very sick person to protect from the "wind." Also, when a normal man suddenly went berserk and killed someone, instead of blaming him, his friends muttered something about the "wind." The translator concluded that in certain contexts "wind" meant "demon." The translator also discovered that they called it "good" because the demon might be listening, and if they called him "evil" it might fly into a rage and harm them. So over the years the accepted word for "demon" had become "the good wind." In the next Bible study, the translator mentioned that Christ could protect them from "the good wind." The reaction was an instanteous and resounding affirmation. They now knew Jesus had power over the forces of evil.[309]

In a somewhat similar case, a translator was trying to discover a suitable word for "spirit" in one of the Aztec dialects. The translator thought he could use a word that had the basic meaning of "evil wind." He imagined that perhaps, with the years, the term had lost its connotation of evil. The word was paired with the Aztec word for "good," but when native speakers heard it used, they simply laughed at the clash of ideas. They still saw the translator as saying in effect, "God's good (evil) spirit." The connotation of evil was implicit in the word regardless of the adjectives placed next to it.[310]

Early one morning Eunice Pike found a headless turkey on her doorstep. She knew what it meant. If someone wanted demons to levy a violent death on an enemy, the turkey was payment for the evil deed. Knowing the power of God, this did not terrify her. In fact Pike used the incident to teach Romans 12:1. She said, "God isn't like the spirits the people say are in the ground. He doesn't want a dead turkey—not even a fat, freshly killed one. He would rather have *us* than a turkey. And, *while we are still alive*, he wants us totally devoted to him and his desires for us."[311]

It is usually not difficult to convince a tribe or people that humans are innately selfish and flawed. They know that, left to themselves, humans tend to do whatever they feel like doing. In the Ndonga

---

309 Pike, *An Uttermost Part*, 104.
310 Beekman and Callow, *Translating the Word of God*, 165.
311 Pike, *An Uttermost Part*, 182.

language, "Everyone did what was right in his own eyes" (Judg 21:25 NASB), is perfectly stated in their proverb "Everyone was a long-grazing goat," presumably meaning "straying wherever they wished."

The Tsongas of South Africa also have a built-in saying about presenting temptation before a person prone to sin. "Do not lead us into temptation": would be rendered, "Do not throw a mouse into a granary of monkey nuts."

Sometimes the accurate word for "temptation" is difficult to identify in a language. Translators in Liberia discovered that they had rendered "lead us not into temptation" (Matt 6:13) as "do not catch us when we sin," a sentiment already appreciated by the Liberians, but now with the added endorsement of scriptural authority.[312]

For months Dorothy James searched for the word "temptation" in the Siane language of Papua New Guinea. She found several close equivalents, including words for "test," but no word for "temptation to sin."

Then one evening a tribesman told a legend about the origin of the moon. In the story, he spoke of people pulling the ear of the main character. When the story was done, Dorothy asked innocently, "Why did they pull that man's ear?"

Her language helper looked at her strangely and began to laugh. "They didn't really grab hold of his ear and pull it," he said. "This is what we say when people talk to someone and try to get him to do something he shouldn't or doesn't want to do." Dorothy finally had her word for temptation.[313]

It is interesting how different languages describe specific sins, sometimes in a way to minimize the evil aspect of it. To the Folopas, if a man or woman wishes to entice the opposite sex, the person says, "Get me!" In Chinantec, Trique, and other Mexican languages, adultery is referred to as "talking to another woman or to another man." In Zoque it is labeled simply "to deceive one's husband or wife." In Ecuador, the Colorado speak of it as "walking with others"; the

---

312 Sanneh, *Translating the Message*, 194.
313 Hefley, *Searchlight on Bible Words*, 184.

Tagabili of the Philippines, as "stepping out on one's partner"; and the Chewa, as "going to have a look at one another."[314]

In the New Testament, yeast often symbolizes corruption or sin. Yeast was a familiar ingredient to people in Jesus' day. But to those in many countries it is only a strange ingredient white-skinned people claim to put into their food. In Mark 8:15 Jesus warned his disciples, "Watch out for the yeast of the Pharisees and that of Herod." At first the disciples thought Jesus was rebuking them for bringing no bread aboard their boat, but he was referring to the corruption hidden within the Pharisees' outward appearance.

Ernest and Marjorie Richert thought long and hard about what word they could use in the Guhu-Samane language in place of "yeast." Finally they chose the word *patta*: "Be on guard with reference to the sour food (*patta*) of the Pharisees and of Herod." What made this word an especially ideal choice is that *patta* is also used to indicate conduct or affairs gone sour.[315]

However, when the Richerts reached Galatians 5:9, "A little yeast works through the whole batch of dough," they did not feel they could use the same word, *patta*, in place of "yeast." Paul was implying the spread of false teachings, and *patta* (sour food) does not spread to other food. Taro—a tuberous, starchy staple of the Guhu-Samanes—is susceptible to a particular blight which strikes a single plant and quickly spreads to others. The tribespeople know they must root out the first infected taro or all the rest will wither. So the translators used the Guhu-Samane example, saying, "If one taro in the garden withers, all the rest will wither."[316]

As Michael Jemphrey translated the epistle to the Galatians into the Supyire language of southern Mali, he also struggled with translating this verse. The making of bread is not unknown in Mali, but it is considered a modern practice. Those living in the bush would not understand what bread is or how yeast relates to it. Unlike certain other Scriptures referring to yeast, the passage surrounding this one does not make the metaphor clear. A similar saying in Mali culture

---

314 Wendland, *The Cultural Factor*, 102.
315 Hefley, *Searchlight on Bible Words*, 38.
316 Ibid., 116–17.

is: "Don't you know that the bean grain which you ignore, nevertheless swells the stomach?" In Supyire this can mean, "The bad words or actions of a single individual can destroy the whole community." Since some in southern Mali are familiar with bread and others are not, at the time of this writing Jemphrey and his team are as yet undecided whether they'll use the yeast illustration literally or substitute the parallel bean saying.[317]

"Yeast" is again used by Paul in 1 Corinthians 5:6,7: "Don't you know that a little yeast works through the whole batch of dough? Get rid of the old yeast." He is challenging the church to get rid of the "yeast" of sin because its affects tend to spread as yeast does through dough. Since the Yaweyuha people know nothing of yeast, Ellis Diebler substituted "pig gall" for "yeast." There is only a small amount of gall in a pig, but if it remains in the dead pig, even when the pig is roasted, the meat retains a bitter flavor.[318]

Neil Anderson was trying to translate Mark 3:27 where Jesus says, "No one can enter a strong man's house and carry off his possessions unless he first ties up the strong man." He explained to the Folopa how Jesus has the power to "tie up" Satan so he cannot dominate us. This did not connect with the Folopa males. In their fighting days, they never tied people up before they plundered their villages. They went only to kill. After all, if they left victims alive, these could identify them to clan brothers, who would exact revenge. Anderson needed another word picture.

A man named Awiame Ali said, "This is like the pythons, like when we catch them." When questioned, Awiame explained that, if given the opportunity, a python could crush the bones of a victim. Hunters must bind the snake first. They grab the python's head and tie leaves about the head with vines. When the snake cannot see, it stops writhing. Then the hunters bind the huge snake to a branch, hoist it on their shoulders, and carry it home for dinner. The Folopa never bind up other humans, but they bind pythons, and this is a word picture with which they could readily identify.[319] Thus,

---

317 Michael Jemphrey, email message to author, August 13, 2002.
318 Ellis Diebler, email message to author, November 20, 2001.
319 Anderson, *In Search*, 105–6.

the figure of speech could read, "No one enters a python's domain without first blinding the snake and binding it."

Of course, in every discussion of temptation and sin there is the distinct possibility of hypocrisy. Though all Christians struggle with the problem of sin, we like to pretend and appear to others that we are morally better than we are.

Desmond Oatridge was finding it difficult locating an expression for "hypocrite" in the Binumarien language. Nothing seemed suitable until one day when he and his language assistant were discussing the hypocrisy of the chief priests. Suddenly the assistant commented, "These chief priests were men of two villages." He explained that a good man would live in and support one village, while a bad man would wander from one village to another, blatantly changing allegiances and cozying up to people wherever he went. So the chief priests here and hypocrites elsewhere in Scripture became "men of two villages."[320]

---

320 Hefley, *Searchlight on Bible Words*, 151.

# CHAPTER FOURTEEN

# For Clarity's Sake

Two of the greatest linguistic challenges for a translator are: (1) to make a Bible translation clear enough for readers to understand, and (2) to discover exactly the right word or phrase to express a biblical idea. These challenges are compounded because the translator is intent on being faithful to two languages, the local people's language with its rules and patterns and the Hebrew or Greek of the original author in the Scripture book to be translated.

This chapter illustrates a wide variety of ways Bible translators have struggled to render Scripture in ways that even those in cultures most diverse from biblical languages and patterns of thinking can understand. Hang on to your hat because our journey will be a brisk one as we hop from one example to the next.

One translator did not think those among the receptor people would understand the words from Mark 1:3, "Prepare the way for the Lord, make straight paths for him." So instead he translated it, "Do good; stop doing bad. The Son of God is coming." This is a very worthy admonition but, the problem is, it is not what Isaiah meant or what Mark recorded in his Gospel.[321]

---

321 Nida, *Language Structure and Translation*.

Another translator couldn't seem to explain to the Zapotec of Sierra Juarez Paul's declaration that a person speaking in unintelligible tongues in the church "will just be speaking into the air" (1 Cor 14:9). He finally discovered that the equivalent expression for "speaking into the air" in Zapotec was literally "speaking into one's own mouth."[322] (If translators don't clarify ideas, they also find themselves "speaking into their own mouths.")

In some of the cultures of the Congo with brutal ways of dealing with their enemies, translators had no idea that the biblical expression "heap coals of fire on one's head" (Rom 12:20) merely sounded to them like an excellent new means of torturing enemy tribespeople.[323]

When translators ask what native word parallels a biblical word, they are sometimes tempted to go with the first option mentioned. In translating the account of the disciples untying the donkey so Jesus could ride it, a translator used a term he understood to mean "unloose." What he didn't know is that the word carried the idea of unloosing with malicious intent. This is why translation projects "make haste slowly," for the unfamiliar words proposed for use in the local language must be thoroughly researched, just as much as the translator digs into the meaning of the original words of Scripture.

Missionaries have realized that even the way a people view the present, past, or future bears on how particular Scriptures must be rendered. For example, the Quechua of Bolivia speak of the future as behind them and the past as ahead of them. Their reasoning is that because one can see in the mind what has already happened, such events must be "in front of one," and that since one cannot see the future, such events must be "behind one."[324]

It is true that "repent" has the idea of reversal, so a translator used a word meaning "reversal," only to learn it was the wrong concept entirely. The term actually meant "to reverse the truth with false testimony to help the accused."

---

322 Beekman and Callow, *Translating the Word of God*, 147.
323 Nida, *Language Structure and Translation*, 43.
324 Ibid., 25.

In the first draft of the Gospel of Mark in the Tonga language, their word *bbiza* (immerse) was used for baptism. This was later rejected because it explicitly excluded the baptismal interpretation of other denominations.[325] Any Baptists involved were no doubt disheartened, but the impreciseness of the Greek word is also the reason English translators rendered the Greek word *baptizo* as "baptize," instead of rendering it either "immerse" or "sprinkle."

A translator thought she'd found the right word for "witnesses" in the Scripture where Jesus tells the apostles they'll be witnesses to him throughout the world. She found out to her chagrin, however, that the word she'd chosen referred only to a court witness who is witnessing for the prosecution.[326]

Another linguist in Central Africa sought to translate the case of Reuben's incest with his father's wife. However, instead of writing that Reuben "defiled his father's bed," in actuality he wrote that Reuben had urinated on his father's bed, an act which made tribesmen think Reuben was either a child or an imbecile.[327]

What does one do with the symbolic dragon in Revelation when translating into Chinese? It's true that some think the dragon in Chinese society represents demonic idol worship, but others believe many Chinese see the dragon as representing good luck and fortune.

And what about the "white robes of the saints" in Revelation? In Korea white is a symbol of mourning, not purity. The idea that saints' robes are made white by "washing them in the blood of the Lamb" can also be confusing. One Filipino concluded on the basis of this verse that it must have been one very weird lamb with no red blood.[328]

A Vietnamese tribesman shook his head when translator Nancy Freiberger read the account from Mark 8 about Jesus healing the deaf and dumb man. "We Nungs would not ever say that a deaf man's ears were opened," he said. "One can open doors, windows, even radios [that's how a Nung turns on a radio], but no one would ever open an ear." Nancy accepted the language helper's judgment.

---

325 Wendland, *The Cultural Factor*, 69.
326 Beekman and Callow, *Translating the Word of God*, 167.
327 Wendland, *The Cultural Factor*, 102.
328 Nida and Reyburn, *Meaning across Cultures*, 2–3.

In the Nung language it reads simply, "Jesus commanded the deaf to 'Hear!' And then he heard."[329]

Translators struggled with Luke 5:39 where Jesus compares people's desire for old wine instead of new to their preference for old, familiar traditions instead of his new truth. One translator in a Cushitic language of East Africa rendered the verse: "When someone drinks beer that has slept some days [fermented], that person does not want new beer that has not yet fermented. He says beer that has slept is best." But the translator wondered if, instead of looking for the symbolic meaning, native people would simply see this as encouragement to drink alcohol.

Wayne Leman acknowledged that alcoholism is also a severe problem where he serves. Besides this, the people do not use or understand metaphors very readily. Thus, Leman tentatively rendered the brief surrounding passage in a very literal way: "Listen to me, you Pharisees and Teachers. How you teach is not the way it is. What I'm teaching is new and is also the truth. If you cling to your own teaching, you will never accept the good way. And when there is teaching, you can't just patch anything here and there. If you listen good to me, you will know how I teach is the only way, and you will be happy."[330]

Some languages are more clear or specific than our English translations, some are less. For example, when it came to translating Christ's feeding of the five thousand in John 6 into the Samo language, the translator had to be very specific about even the type of grass the crowds sat upon. Seem irrelevant? In Samo there are two general types of grass, then many specific types classified according to growing patterns, amount of seeds, what they are used for, etc. This could be important simply because, if the wrong type of grass is named, the Samo might become distracted or incredulous, knowing, for example, that people would never sit down on a particular type of grass.[331]

---

329 Hefley, *Searchlight on Bible Words*, 144.
330 Wayne Leman, email message to author, March 14, 2002.
331 D. Shaw, *Transculturation*, 155.

Speaking of specificity, the Chol language has no generic term for "to carry," but it uses a number of particular terms indicating whether an item is carried on the back, on the shoulder, in the arms, with the hand, or even with the finger. Conversely, in a Philippine language, ants, crocodiles, foxes, and cobras are grouped together under one generic word based on the fact that they bite.[332] And in Vietnamese, to "eat rice" can refer to a meal without rice, and the word "rice" can be used to refer to other types of grain. If it is vital that a reader know which kind of grain, a picture of the grain variety can be shown.[333]

Translators never imagined that the phrase "months gone by" was not appropriate in the Chewa language. Chewas would say "the time of yesterday's mother."[334]

Translators also had a problem when translating the statement from Ruth 2:7: "She . . . worked steadily . . . except for a short rest in the shelter." They learned belatedly that the Chewa expression "in the house she doesn't stay long" meant that Ruth was either a busybody or a loose woman.[335]

There are many Scriptures that translators have had to make slightly more personal or specific for the sake of clarity. Some examples follow:

> Mark 4:17: "They have no root" becomes "The Word does not take root in them."
>
> Acts 15:10: "Why do you try to test God by putting on the necks of the disciples a yoke . . .?" becomes "Why do you tempt God by asking the disciples to do something very difficult . . .?"
>
> James 3:6: "The tongue also is a fire," becomes "What we say ruins people like a fire ruins things."[336]

At times, uniquely biblical words must be identified by a newly constructed word or a string of words. For example, the Passover has

---

[332] Beekman and Callow, *Translating the Word of God*, 185.
[333] Ibid., 188.
[334] Wendland, *The Cultural Factor*, 131.
[335] Ibid., 173.
[336] Beekman and Callow, *Translating the Word of God*, 146–50.

been rendered "the feast at which they ate sheep," "the Jewish feast about God delivering them," or "the feast remembering when God's angel passed by." As is obvious, some descriptive phrases touch at the heart of Passover's meaning while others fall slightly short.[337]

Jean Goddard and her partner faced a similar problem when they were translating the Gospel of Mark for the Agarabi tribe. They did not know how to translate the word "Passover" in Mark 14:1. After telling their Agarabi language helper the background story from Exodus, he recalled for them the old days when their warriors might bypass one village to attack a third. They decided that the Agarabi word for "bypass" was close enough to use for the word "Passover," since God passed over the firstborn of the Israelites on that fateful night.[338]

Many believers view the sacrifice of the lamb at Passover as a foreshadowing of what Christ would do centuries later as the Lamb of God. However, when a person is compared to a sheep, it can mean very different things in different cultures. It has been found to mean a long-haired man, a drunkard, a person who doesn't answer back, one who just follows without thinking, or a young man waiting for girls to chase him.[339]

In cultures where sheep are completely unknown, translators must be careful about what animal they might introduce in their place. At first glance, for the Eskimos, seals might be a natural equivalent to lambs. However, seals differ radically from sheep in the culture. For example, in some parts of Scripture, humans are compared to sheep in regard to their tendency to stray, the need to be specially protected and cared for, etc. Among Eskimos, seals are not farmed or protected and therefore do not stray; they are hunted. This does not comprise a suitable functional equivalent.

When another linguist substituted "horse" for "sheep" in a translation for horse-loving Indians of Canada, missionary colleagues objected to the substitution. They felt that a substitution should not

---

337 Ibid., 192.
338 Hefley, *Searchlight on Bible Words*, 57.
339 Larson, *Meaning-based Translation*, 251.

be made simply because an animal is esteemed more highly in a given culture.[340]

In Job 13:12, Job tells his friends, "Your maxims are proverbs of ashes; your defenses are defenses of clay." However, in the Tonga culture this didn't make sense: ashes are valuable in making soap, fertilizer, and an insecticide, and clay isn't considered weak; it makes solid pots and strengthens the foundation of homes. Translators decided to substitute "dust" for "ashes" and "sand" for "clay."[341]

Occasionally the string of words replacing one biblical word can become distressingly lengthy. In the Lalana Chinantec language of Mexico, to "cast lots" is expressed "playing with little round things which make it evident who will be favored."[342] And the Peruvian Shipibos have never played any games of chance, so the whole concept must be explained in the verse (i.e. Luke 23:34).

Similarly, where Jesus rebukes the Pharisees for making their phylacteries broad, it required a lot of words to explain to the Chewa people that Pharisees do things for the sake of show—things such as "enlarging small satchels containing the word of God which they wear on their forehead and wrist."[343]

John 1:17 states that "grace and truth came through Jesus Christ." Since grace and truth form the subject of "came," the Trique Indians assumed that Grace and Truth must be two angels Christ sent to earth. The phrase needed to read something like, "Jesus Christ was full of grace and truth."[344]

Saying that Jesus "told them plainly" (John 11:14) does not communicate clearly in the Chewa language. Chewas would say, "Jesus smashed the matter" (like a gourd).[345]

The English word "angel" is not a translation, but rather a transliteration of the Greek. Translator David Foris also realized that the Spanish word for "angel" just magnified the confusion among the

---

340 Nida and Reyburn, *Meaning across Cultures*, 55.
341 Wendland, *The Cultural Factor*, 116.
342 Beekman and Callow, *Translating the Word of God*, 196.
343 Wendland, *The Cultural Factor*, 65.
344 Beekman and Callow, *Translating the Word of God*, 221.
345 Wendland, *The Cultural Factor*, 131.

Sochiapan Chinantec Indians. The Spanish term implied the idea that the stars are both the spirits of dead babies as well as angels.

While casting about for a possible term for "angel," Foris happened to ask the identity of the new village authorities. He was told the name of the president. Then the individual said, "And the president's people-hands and people-feet are . . . [his elected officials]. Foris suddenly had a brainstorm. Since angels are God's workers or messengers, could they be referred to as the "people-hands, people-feet" of God? When Foris tried the idea on a few translation assistants, they agreed. Angels, like town officials, are under authority but are also lent some authority by God himself. The phrase seemed to work.[346]

Many times issues pertaining to the human body are not clearly translated into a receptor language. For example, in the King James Bible, Saul was said to have entered a cave to "cover his feet" (1 Sam 24:3). This would lead us to believe maybe his feet were cold or he was ready for sleep. But this phrase literally means to "relieve one's bowels." The first Bible translation into the Chewa erroneously stated that Saul went in to warm his feet. The Chewa idiom for relieving oneself is "to help oneself," so that's how the revised Chewa translation of the verse was rendered.[347]

Dr. Eugene Nida often checked translations for accuracy. There was a problem with Acts 14:8 as rendered in the Mazatec language. Reading that the man in Lystra was a cripple "from his mother's womb" (NASB), Mazatecs assumed that the mother's womb caused the injury. Nida suggested simply rendering the phrase, "being a cripple ever since he was born." Nida always emphasized the fact that it was the meaning and message translators were supposed to get across, not just the words.[348]

Conversely, when in Genesis 38:15 the Tumbukas of Malawi found Judah assuming his own daughter-in-law to be a prostitute because she had her face covered, this was very confusing because

---

346 David Foris, email message to author, November 28, 2001.
347 Wendland, *The Cultural Factor*, 22.
348 Pike, *Words Wanted*, 96.

covering the face is only the normal response of a respectful woman in the presence of her father-in-law.[349]

While studying the book of Ruth, a Nigerian student commented frequently about how similar his culture was to the way they did things during this period. The importance of the levirate, the kinsman redeemer, and the functions of inheritance all had parallels in his culture.[350]

However, Chewa readers assumed that when Naomi instructed Ruth to wash, perfume, dress up, and go to where Boaz was, she was teaching her how to be enticing as a prostitute so Ruth could earn enough money to support them both.[351] In the same vein, in the Higi culture, if a widow approached Boaz the way Ruth did, she would be severely reprimanded. But translator Dan Shaw believes it would violate biblical context in this case if Ruth's behavior was changed to the way a Higi woman would have behaved. Instead, Shaw believes the passage should be rendered as is, with an appropriate indication that this behavior was acceptable in Jewish culture.[352] Translators must be careful to avoid misunderstandings such as this.

Linguist Neil Anderson was trying to translate into Folopa the fact that the ground had been cursed because of mankind's sin. He added that humans would eat bread only by the sweat of their brow. The Folopa were puzzled by this verse. Then Anderson realized that in the tropics the people perspired *constantly*; they dripped sweat just sitting in their houses. When Anderson asked how they might say this verse, a man said, "We speak of bursting our stomach." Anderson realized this was similar to the English slang, "busting a gut." The verse was translated, "No longer will your food just come up by itself, but by bursting your stomach you will do your work and raise your food" (Gen 3:19).

Later in his translation of Genesis, Anderson came to the passage in which Potiphar's wife tried to seduce Joseph. He explained that the woman trapped Joseph in the house. In Folopa culture, the men sleep

---

349 Wendland, *The Cultural Factor*, 109.
350 John Guli, "The Book of Ruth in Higi" (unpublished manuscript, Fuller Seminary School of World Mission, Pasadena, CA, 1984).
351 Wendland, *The Cultural Factor*, 177–78.
352 D. Shaw, *Transculturation*, 102.

in separate quarters from the women. In addition, there is virtually no privacy in the village, no place for couples to get intimate. The garden or the cover of the bush is the only place for privacy and intimacy. So things seemed perplexingly reversed when Potiphar's wife seduced Joseph in the house after which he fled into the "bush."[353]

After translating Paul's words, "For one believeth that he may eat all things: another, who is weak, eateth herbs" (Rom 14:2 KJV), a linguist heard readers claiming that this person must be physically weak, since he had taken to eating herbs for his health. The linguist had to be very clear in the translation: "One believes that he may eat all things. Another, who is weak in faith, believes that he should eat only herbs."[354]

In Luke 12:54,55 Jesus says, "When you see a cloud rising in the west, immediately you say, 'It's going to rain,' and it does. And when the south wind blows, you say, 'It's going to be hot,' and it is." However, these descriptions are peculiar to Palestine and would sound inaccurate to speakers of languages where the rain or heat emanate from other directions. Thus, it would be advisable to preface Christ's description of the weather with "Here" or "In this country."[355]

In the Chewa language the sole word for "grave" is *manda* (dug down into the earth). Since their "tombs" were holes, it was mystifying that Christ accused people of being like whitewashed tombs. Similarly the word for "boat" in Tonga means a canoe holding only two or three persons at a time. Thus, tribesmen didn't find it at all surprising that when Jesus and his disciples all climbed into one boat, it was soon in danger of being swamped.[356]

The closest substitute for "chariot" in Chewa was the term meaning "ox cart." However, it was very hard for them to believe that Pharaoh and his army overtook the Israelites in a collection of ox carts.[357]

The Genesis account of Laban's angry pursuit of Jacob includes a scene in which his daughter Rachel refuses to allow her father to

---

353 Anderson, *In Search*, 57–59.
354 Beekman and Callow, *Translating the Word of God*, 47.
355 Ibid., 57.
356 Wendland, *The Cultural Factor*, 72.
357 Ibid., 73.

search her camel's saddle for house gods because "the manner of women is upon me" (Gen 31:35 NASB). An equivalent expression in Chewa for menstruation is "I cannot salt the stew." This euphemism seemed appropriate until a rampant animistic superstition was recounted to the effect that if a menstruating woman cooked stew it would cause a mysterious swelling disease among the family.[358]

The parable of the lost coin (Luke 15:8–10) was translated into Muong, a language and culture of Vietnam. For the coins that the woman lost, translators used a general word for "coin." But when the Muong read it, they were rather incredulous that anyone would go to all the trouble of sweeping the house to find money of such little value. It needed to made explicit in the story that the coins were *worth* searching for.[359]

On the other hand, in some languages it is possible to make Scripture too explicit. In certain Peruvian languages, every time the proper name "God" was used in the Creation narrative, it meant that an additional god was involved in the creative process. The name God was to be used once in the story, and thereafter referred to by pronoun.[360]

A translator found that there was no specific word for "blaspheme" in the Filipino Manobo language of the Philippines. He decided to engineer a new word based on the Manobo vocabulary. First he found the word for criticize and modified this to arrive at the expression "to criticize by speech." This triggered his language helper's understanding of what they were looking for, and he came up with about eight words for different ways of criticizing someone. From these words the translator found significant components so as to finally express the idea of blasphemy clearly.[361]

Graham and Margaret Scott were translating the Bible for the Fore tribe of the Eastern Highlands of Papua New Guinea. When they came to Mark 10:31, "Many who are first will be last, and the last first," the Fore language helper said, "That's easy to translate:

---

358 Ibid., 79.
359 Beekman and Callow, *Translating the Word of God*, 61.
360 Ibid., 65.
361 Ibid., 72–73.

Those who follow the Lord first will be the last to go up to heaven, and those who follow him last will go up first."

The Scotts had to explain that this was not exactly what Jesus meant. The helper understood when they translated the verse as, "Many who are leaders will be nothing-people, and nothing-people will be the leaders."[362]

It is obvious that many concepts of language are uniquely tied to culture. 1 Thessalonians 5:21 cautions against false teaching and challenges Christians to test or try such instruction. The idea of testing would be foreign to the Navajo. A more clear rendering reads: "Track down all kinds of teaching," as in tracking a horse or a thief until he is found.[363]

An unexpectedly difficult question arose when translating "Aaron's rod which budded" (Hebrews 9:4 NASB). The translation assistant had to know what kind of tree the rod was fashioned from. He even had to know the color of the blossoms. In Navajo there is great specificity in nature; there are many words for "bud," and even the color of particular buds is incorporated into the word used.[364]

In one of the Eskimo languages, the root of the words used for "generations" and "descendants" is the same as that of the word for the long rope attached from the lead dog to the sled. Just as all the dogs are harnessed to the same rope as the lead dog, human descendants of a family form one long chain.[365]

It's interesting how 2 Timothy 2:17 reads in the Hopi Indian language. In the King James Version it reads, "And their word will eat as doth a canker." A canker was similar to a carbuncle, and the Hopi word for "carbuncle" meant "an anthill sore." "Their words will become like an anthill sore," reads the Hopi verse.

A translator's helper came to Mark 1:6, "And John was clothed with camel's hair, and with a girdle of skin about his loins; and he did eat locusts and wild honey," and read his rendition in Mazatec.

The helper asked, "Whose land was the honey on?"

---

362 Hefley, *Searchlight on Bible Words*, 147.
363 Wallis, *God Speaks Navajo*, 106.
364 Ibid., 107.
365 Ibid., 115.

The translator blanched. Was this young upstart calling John a thief? "Those bees were not near someone's house," he sputtered.

"I own land," said the helper. "It was my father's. It is land where no one is and it has bees there."

The translator tried again, "I don't know whose land this was. It may not have been John's land."

"Then this translation is not right," said the helper simply. "It sounds like John owned the land."[366]

Wayne and Betty Snell faced formidable problems when translating Acts into the Machiguenga language of southeastern Peru. Many terms had no single-word equivalent in the Machiguenga language, so the Snells had to improvise for the sake of clarity. There was no word for "city," so they indicated that this was where many houses were grouped together. The Machiguengas had never seen an ocean, so the Mediterranean was referred to as a large lake. "Temple" and "synagogue" had no equivalents in this language. "Temple" was translated as "God's house" and "synagogue" was the place where the Jews gather together repeatedly.[367]

Old Testament language speaks of a person "lifting up his eyes." Translating the idiom literally in one Middle Eastern language means to pick them up off a table, and in an Oriental language it means to roll them back in the head as in a trance. Other questions arise in the minds of native speakers. Is comparing Ishmael to a wild ass a compliment or a gross insult? Does the phrase "The Lord is my rock" mean he makes you stumble or that he is a shelter? And does the clause "he ties his young donkey to a grapevine and washes his garment in wine" mean that the man is an ignorant bachelor or that he's filthy rich?[368]

Translator Jim Loriot was seeking to translate the verse about John the Baptist leaping in his mother's womb (Luke 1:41). When the language informant read the word Loriot had used for "leap," he indicated this would be unclear to the people.

---

366 Ibid., 29.
367 Nida and Reyburn, *Meaning across Cultures*, 64.
368 Hefley, *Searchlight on Bible Words*, 34.

"Fleas, grasshoppers, and one kind of frog leap in this way," he said, "but human beings or large animals never leap."

"What do babies do when they move suddenly in the womb?" asked Jim.

The Indian grinned. "They play."

So Loriot rendered the verse: "The babe played in her womb."

Neil Anderson hit a bump while translating the parable of the good Samaritan. When he tried to describe the wounds of the victim, he could discover no word for "wound" in Folopa. This may seem like a trivial issue, but linguists are committed to translating the Scriptures as thoroughly as possible, being as literal as understanding allows.

The Folopas asked, "What weapon was used?"

Anderson said, "I don't know. What does it matter?"

But the Folopas insisted.

Finally Anderson said, "Well, what if it was a spear? A dagger? An axe?"

"No," they kept saying. "These weapons would outright kill the man."

"How about arrows?"

"No, he would have pulled them out. Does your Book say he pulled arrows?"

"Well," said Anderson, exasperated, "what if they just beat him with their hands?"

"No, that would not have left open wounds."

Anderson was almost ready to give up when the Folopas ventured a possibility. "If the man was beaten with clubs, he could have wounds."

Translating it this way, Anderson was able to get across that there were open wounds into which the Samaritan poured his medicine.[369]

---

369 Anderson, *In Search*, 135–37.

CHAPTER FIFTEEN

# Hard Sayings

WHEN PEOPLE HEAR THE STORY OF CHRIST in their language for the first time, they don't always receive it with open arms. In fact, the Gugu-Yalanji people of the Australian desert were downright offended with Jesus.

The translator described in their language how Jesus had disagreed with the scribes and Pharisees.

"Jesus was wrong," they objected. "He should never have disagreed with the old men."

They said that in going against the elders Jesus was committing a very serious offense. The translator pointed out that the scribes and Pharisees weren't following the law as given by God at the first. Instead, they'd changed that law and established their own. Jesus was following God's original law and expressing the spirit of that law.

Still, the Gugu-Yalanjis were not convinced. When they learned of Jesus' death, some actually concluded that it was a logical punishment for speaking against the elders.

The translator realized that, until hearts were changed, the tribespeople would continue to judge scriptural stories solely by their own tribal stories, laws, and customs.[370]

---

370 Hefley, *Searchlight on Bible Words*, 49.

There are other aspects of Christ's life which can easily be misunderstood. In some areas of West Africa the action of putting branches in the path of an oncoming chief as the crowds did for Jesus would be considered a gross insult. Sometimes, however, these Africans have been known to sweep the path when a dignitary is coming to visit. Thus, in the Christ account, the crowds could be said to sweep Jesus' path with branches.[371]

Another potential area of confusion was Christ's relationship to women. For example, when Jesus addressed Mary as "woman" following his resurrection (John 20:25), he could be falsely understood to be addressing her as his wife.[372] Similarly, in some African languages, when Jesus asked the Samaritan woman for a drink, it may be understood as making a request for sexual relations. To avoid misunderstanding, a translator could write: "Being thirsty, Jesus said to her, 'Give me a drink of water.'"[373]

A Thai congregation struggled to understand Christ's response to the Gentile woman who requested healing for her demon-possessed daughter. Christ's initial refusal and seeming ridicule of the woman as a dog confused the Thai, and they concluded the Christian faith must be neurotic. In other cultures and other times, it has been the "assault" or testing of the woman's faith that's been the focus of the passage, but in Buddhist Bangkok the focus was more appropriately the initiation of faith budding from a mother's love for her child.[374]

Philippine tribesmen misunderstood when they heard the parable of the prodigal son. They were convinced that what happened to the son was totally the fault of the father who should have known better than to give his younger son his portion of the estate early. Also, some Papua tribesmen could not view the experience of the son in the far country as degrading. In their rural society, feeding many pigs is a very prestigious vocation.[375]

---

371 Nida and Reyburn, *Meaning across Cultures*, 73.
372 Ibid., 80.
373 Ibid., 73.
374 Kosuke Koyama, "Thailand: Points of Theological Friction," in *Asian Voices in Christian Theology*, ed. Gerald H. Anderson (Maryknoll, NY: Orbis Books, 1976), 73–75.
375 Nida and Waard, *One Language to Another*, 76.

The Folopa were certain the translation of Luke 14:26 was wrong when they read the statement by Jesus: "Unless a person hates his father, mother, wife, children, and all, he cannot be my disciple."

Among the Folopa, clan ties and family ties are almost unbreakable. One will do anything for a blood brother. So, naturally, they thought the verse should read not *"unless"* but *"if* a person hates . . . he cannot be my disciple."

Days of fruitless controversy ensued. Neil Anderson admitted that Jesus does not teach people to hate, but he couldn't figure out how to explain this quotation by Jesus. It didn't help at all to dilute the verse: "Unless you hate your clansmen just a little bit, you cannot be my disciple."

At length, Anderson was able to communicate that when it comes down to a contest of allegiance, God must win. "It may appear," he told clansmen, "in the eyes of your family and clansmen that you hate them. That will happen because you'll be doing what God wants and not what they want."

A man named Wheare glimpsed the light. He said, "Jesus was not saying we're supposed to hate our families or our clansmen or anyone else. In following him there will be times when we act in such a way that they imagine that because we follow God's will instead of theirs, we must hate them."

Finally they understood.[376]

Occasional biblical ideas cause confusion, even misgivings, in receptor cultures. The Old Testament concept of the "uncleanness" of menstruating women seems strange in societies where menstruation is very positive as a symbol of fertility. Christ's "coming in the clouds" is disconcerting in parts of the Orient where a person associated with clouds would be a troublemaker. The Indian prejudice against eating beef has moved some translators to argue that, in cases such as Abraham's roasting of a calf for his heavenly visitors, the beef should be switched to roast lamb. And the playing of flutes at a Middle Eastern funeral (Matt 9:23) causes those of some cultures to wonder if the occasion was actually a pleasurable experience.[377]

---

[376] Anderson, *In Search*, 166–70.
[377] Nida and Reyburn, *Meaning across Cultures*, 50–52.

Some Navajo words are extremely similar. For example, the words for "altar" (that on which something is offered) and for "counter" (upon which something is sold) only differ in the length of one vowel and the tone used. Once, when reading the term "altar" in Matthew's Gospel, a Navajo group misinterpreted the term as "counter." They became very angry. Years before, the government had determined that the range on the Navajo reservation was overgrazed, so they ordered the Indians to trade their sheep at *counters* in trading posts. Large numbers of sheep were sacrificed to the government for little compensation. A hatred developed for that project and for the whites involved. The translator had to teach the tribespeople to read their own language carefully, noting subtle differences between words and phrases.[378]

When Kungbushmen learned of various biblical characters who fasted, they were indignant. First, they knew every good gift was from this Creator God. In their culture, whenever someone refused a gift, it was a gross insult to the giver. Thus, refusing to eat what God had obviously provided for human survival and well being was an inexcusable affront to him. They found it very difficult to accept that fasting was meant to reflect contrition or repentance or allow for more focused prayer and worship.[379]

The Folopa loved hearing the translation of the book of Acts. The males especially exulted in the courage of the ordinary, unschooled apostles as they stood against the powerful leaders. The apostles had God on their side; miracles and angelic assistance rendered them unstoppable.

Then the unbelievable happened. The apostles were flogged.

The Folopas said, "That can't be right. Are you sure you have the right word?"

Anderson rechecked it. Yes, it was "flog," as in "strike."

The clansmen were stunned.

Anderson continued reading, "The apostles left the Sanhedrin, rejoicing because they had been counted worthy of suffering disgrace for the Name" (Acts 5:41).

---

378 Wallis, *God Speaks Navajo*, 105–6.
379 Nida and Waard, *One Language to Another*, 76.

Flogging was not an honor; it was a shame. How could God allow his heroes to be beaten? And how could these apostles possibly rejoice in such total disgrace? Clansmen began silently to leave the room. This was too much.

It became one of the hardest biblical concepts Anderson ever tackled at the translation desk. The Folopa couldn't understand the paradox. It was like getting a report card in which the teacher says, "You've done very well, so I've decided to give you an F." Or like a boss saying, "You're doing a great job; you're fired." Some never quite grasped the idea.[380]

Similarly, the Guiaica of Venezuela went ballistic when Jesus refused to fight against or flee from those who came to arrest him. Among the Guiaica, a man in danger who didn't attack or try a daring escape would be either a coward or insane.[381] And a Buddhist interpreted Christ's healing of blind Bartimaeus as a curse rather than a blessing. In the Buddhist mindset, the man was better off not seeing all the evil and ugly misery of human existence.[382]

---

380 Anderson, *In Search*, 180–81.
381 Nida and Reyburn, *Meaning across Cultures*, 48.
382 Ibid.

CHAPTER SIXTEEN

# Translators Laugh (at Themselves) Too

B<small>IBLE TRANSLATORS ARE GENERALLY VERY NICE PEOPLE</small>. They're even cool enough to sit back now and then and have a good long laugh at the inevitable misunderstandings and mistakes of translation work that arise when crossing language and cultural boundaries.

Linguists must be meticulous about issues such as spelling, accent marks, and tonal identifiers. In the Pitjantjatjara language of the western desert of Australia, the word for "life" has an "n" sound which is produced with the tongue tip on the gum ridge. To inadvertently place the tongue tip behind the gum ridge and toward the roof of the mouth produces the word meaning "hairy processionary caterpillar." Without appropriate accents, John 6:47 would be understood to mean, "He that believes on me has hairy processionary caterpillars." This was not good news at all to these Aboriginal people. When handled, processionary caterpillars caused an irritating, burning skin rash.

In the same language, failure to place the tongue between the teeth when trying to say the word for "son" results in the word for "head" instead. Imagine how hearers would react to the story of the prodigal son: "A certain man had two heads" (Luke 15:11).[383]

Missionaries in East Africa were fit to be tied when they learned that for fifty years they'd been using words that implied, "The Lord be with your spirit because we sure don't want him."

Ellis Diebler, translator to the Gahuku people of New Guinea, illustrates how easy it is for a translation to convey the wrong meaning. He was translating the call of Jesus in Mark 1:15: "Repent ye, and believe the gospel" (KJV). "Gospel" means "good news," so he decided to render it, "Repent and believe the good new talk." Then he discovered that "new talk" is a Gahuku idiom meaning "a lie." He'd been telling people to repent and believe the good lie![384] And when another translator came to the reference in Revelation 13:15 in which breath is given to the image, he mistakenly translated it, "He made the image stink."[385]

Obviously, both translators were thoroughly embarrassed.

Similarly, Maurice and Helen Boxwell thought they'd found an appropriate word for "shield" in Genesis 15:1: "Do not be afraid, Abram. I am your shield." They learned a word for something Weri males carried to protect themselves when fighting. When Weris drew the object, it even looked like a shield. However, following more questions, the Boxwells learned that the village sorcerer made the object as a charm to be hung from warriors' ears during a battle. They could not have God saying to Abram, "I am your lucky charm." But if the Boxwells had not been so inquisitive, this is exactly what they would have written.[386]

Kitty and Leslie Pride struggled a bit when trying to translate the Scripture in Matthew 6 about praying in one's closet into the Chatino language. First, they discovered they were saying people should leave their house to pray. Then they were told they were instructing Chatinos to go pray in a house just out of town. When they tried to translate the idea of praying with one's Father in secret, they discovered that the secret place they were assigning to God was

---

383 Hefley, *Searchlight on Bible Words*, 22.
384 Nida, *Language Structure and Translation*, 189.
385 Hefley, *Searchlight on Bible Words*, 22–23.
386 Nida, *God's Word*, 43.

a little drawer under an altar table. Translating accurately is not always easy.[387]

The Apostle Paul makes a point in 1 Corinthians 9:5 that apostles have the perfect right to be accompanied by a wife on their journeys. However, one translator's rendition of the verse read literally, "Do we not have the right to lead a wife around like an ox?"[388] And in West Africa, linguists were humiliated when they learned they'd translated the story of Mary sitting at the feet of Jesus unwittingly with the implication that Mary was sitting in Jesus' lap!

Translators had to be careful with the Middle Eastern expression "gnashing at him with their teeth." In one culture it was assumed that the crowd was literally "chewing on him." Interestingly, in the Yao language they use a similar expression for "gnashing" which means "having itchy teeth."[389]

There are also times when translators can't make sense out of native idioms. For example, among the Uduks of Sudan, what we call the "Adam's apple" they call "the thing that loves beer." When you think about it, though, is their expression any stranger than ours?[390]

One's context had better be very clear when using one of the two words for "fruit" in the Kaka (Yamba) language of Cameroon. There are two generic words for "fruit": one includes only bananas and pineapples, and the other includes all other kinds of fruit, plus testicles, glands, kidneys, hearts, soccer balls, pills, and the seed of any fruit or plant.[391]

In some cases, biblical figures of speech can be literally translated into a new language and simply explained by translators to the people or described in footnotes or glossary items. In other cases, a figure of speech will come across nonsensically in another language. The Chol language in quite literal. A "house divided against itself" cannot possibly refer to the occupants, and Chols assume a "sin against heaven" must be a sin against the sky. If a translator were to invite the Chol

---

387 Hefley, *Searchlight on Bible Words*, 171.
388 Ibid., 135.
389 Nida, *God's Word*, 44.
390 Nida and Reyburn, *Meaning across Cultures*, 55–56.
391 Ibid., 1.

to "come under his roof," he'd be understood to mean his house is only partially built.[392]

George and Florence Cowan were translating the book of James into the Huautla Mazatec dialect of Mexico. When they reached James 3:11, they read in the King James Version: "Doth a fountain send forth at the same place sweet water and bitter?" To their amusement, the Cowans found that in Huautla "sweet water" means "soda pop" and "bitter water" means "beer." They knew the translation couldn't exactly read: "Does a fountain send forth at the same place soda pop and beer?" They retained the original meaning by rendering the verse, "A water hole—from that one place does clean, fresh water and salt water come out?"[393]

When translators Phillip and Mary Baer read Mark 12:38,40, "Beware of the scribes . . . who devour widows' houses" (NASB), they faced a problem. Among the Lacandon people of Mexico, animals and jungle termites literally *do* devour the palm roofs and houses of the Indians. Thus, if they read of scribes eating womens' homes, they could only conclude that a scribe is either some species of animal or insect or a strange human who finds dried palm appetizing! So the Baers decided to translate the portion simply: "Beware of the scribes . . . who take the possessions of widows and use them up."[394]

In 2 Samuel 16:16 Hushai says to Absalom, "Long live the king!" This is literally how certain translators rendered it, and the language helper acknowledged that readers would possibly be able to grasp the idea. However, he reported that this wasn't the way his people would say it. In Tonga they would say, "*Aaongole mwami!*" (May the chief live to be bent over in his back). They are not wishing a crippling case of rheumatoid arthritis on their chief. It's just their way of expressing hope that he'll live to be a very old man.[395]

When Seymour Ashley began translating Christ's parable of the vineyard (Matthew 21) into the Filipino Tausug language, he wondered how to interpret the statement that the vineyard owner went into a far country. Ashley asked his assistant, "If the owner of the

---

392 Nida, *Language Structure and Translation*, 41.
393 Hefley, *Searchlight on Bible Words*, 180.
394 Ibid., 116.
395 Wendland, *The Cultural Factor*, 27.

vineyard didn't give his destination, didn't say how long he planned to stay or when he was returning. How would you say that?"

The Filipino said, "We would say, 'he paddled.'"

This didn't surprise Ashley. The Tausug earn their very living from the sea. But he told the assistant, "Sorry, this man in the parable didn't travel on a boat."

"That doesn't matter," came the answer. "We use this word even if we go by truck or on foot."

So in the Tausug language, the vineyard owner "paddled to a far country."[396]

In English, when drivers slow down on an interstate highway to gawk at an accident, we call it "rubbernecking." The Mazatecs use a somewhat similar expression to mean something different. To them miracles are known as "long-necked things" because they stir people's curiosity and crowds "stretch their necks" to see what is happening.[397]

For centuries the Waoranis of South America were cannibalistic, so, of course, though Christ had changed their hearts, they still remembered those days clearly. In fact, when they came to the story of Herodias' daughter asking for the head of John the Baptist on a platter, a Waorani named Dawa said, *"Kewa wado!"* (Cannibals, I'm sure!). Why else, he figured, would they want John's head on a platter?[398]

Surely translators were flabbergasted when they learned that their translation of John 1:1 read: "In the beginning there was *palaver* (idle chatter), and the *idle chatter* was with God, and the *idle chatter was* God."[399]

Further along in the same passage, a translator wished to communicate that the Word was "full of grace and truth" (John 1:14). The word used for "grace" in the native language meant "a living gift." However, since the only "living gifts" people exchanged in the

---

396 Hefley, *Searchlight on Bible Words*, 175.
397 Sanneh, *Translating the Message*, 195.
398 Hefley, *Searchlight on Bible Words*, 165.
399 Sanneh, *Translating the Message*, 193.

culture were chickens, the people understood the phrase to mean "full of chicken and truth."[400]

In 2 Samuel 10 we read that the allies of Syria, who'd been soundly beaten by David, sued for peace with Israel. The natural way of communicating in Tonga what the allies did would be to say they *zyakabaloka* (dropped their loincloths), or *bakakeempa* (blew their noses). Either phrase means that, due to shame or sorrow, they no longer wanted to do any more fighting.[401]

Concepts of physical attractiveness differ from one culture to another. In Stephen's final sermon in Jerusalem he described the child Moses as lovely or beautiful. Karl and Joice Franklin were wondering how to translate "lovely" into the Kewa language of Papua New Guinea. Kewa tribespeople said Moses must have had a nose with a bridge going on and on. The Kewas associate facial attractiveness with a long, slender nose, rather than one *cut short, lifted up abruptly,* or *spread all over the face.*[402]

There are other cultural ideas that may not be particularly attractive to us in the West. Throughout the Bible, oil is often named as something with soothing and curative powers. However, the Gugu-Yalanji people do not prefer this method of healing. They told translators Henry and Ruth Hershberger that the disciples should have rubbed the sick with perspiration from under the healer's arm. This, they said, gives the sick person strength from the healer to overcome illness. The Hershbergers might well have drawn the line when it came to rendering verses such as James 5:14, "Is any one of you sick? He should call the elders of the church to pray over him and anoint him with underarm perspiration in the name of the Lord."[403]

The Bora people live along the Putumayo River on the boundary between Colombia and Peru. When translators came to Acts 20:37, which relates the emotional farewell given Paul by the Ephesian elders, the Bora culture did not permit a literal rendering of the verse. To say that "they all wept as they embraced him and kissed him" was very unrealistic and inappropriate in the Bora culture. Their idea of

---

400 Nida, *God's Word*, 48.
401 Wendland, *The Cultural Factor*, 105.
402 Hefley, *Searchlight on Bible Words*, 17.
403 Ibid., 52.

a truly affectionate farewell is to embrace a friend and to smell him. We Westerners may recoil at this idea, but is placing our wet lips on other people's faces any less strange?[404]

In Cuicateco "the Baptist" is considered John's last name and indicates nothing about his ministry. Thus, in local conversation he was distinguished from John the Apostle with the phrase, "John Baptist, who watered people."[405] And in the Bakau language of Gambia, John was referred to as "John, the Swimmer." With the Atlantic Ocean at their doorstep, the Bakaus may have perceived John as a superhuman swimmer.[406]

Occasionally translators borrow words from a central language in order to get across difficult concepts. This must be practiced with caution, though, because sometimes native preachers use loanwords which carry little meaning or even false meaning to them or their listeners.

In one such case, *alabar* (to worship) was borrowed from Spanish. However, the translator had to clarify when he discovered that the Mazahuas were interpreting the word as *a lavar* (to wash). Since their own idol gods sometimes needed to be washed, the idea of "washing God" sounded logical enough.[407]

A young tribesman in Ghana volunteered to help with Bible translation work. He said he'd heard the Bible taught in his language, but it had often been mispronounced and had resulted in quite a bit of confusion among his people. For example, the word for "road" in his Kusai dialect was almost the same as the word for "soup." He had always wondered why Paul walked in the soup on his journey to Damascus.[408]

A young Indian evangelist was heard quoting Jesus from Mark 2:11 as saying, "Arise, take up your milk, and go to your house." This was because of the similarity of the word *leche* (milk) and the word *lecho* (bed).[409]

---

404 Ibid., 117.
405 Beekman and Callow, *Translating the Word of God*, 199.
406 Sanneh, *Translating the Message*, 193.
407 Beekman and Callow, *Translating the Word of God*, 200.
408 Hefley, *Searchlight on Bible Words*, 187.
409 William Wheeler, Dwight Day, and James Rodgers, *Modern Missions in Mexico* (Philadelphia: Westminster Press, 1925), 262–64.

In a translation of Christ's temptation in the Chewa language, the "highest point of the temple" where Christ was taken by Satan (Matt 4:5; Luke 4:9) was rendered with the word *chimbudzi*, meaning "the topmost, central tuft of a round house." A very similar word, *chimbuzi*, means "an outdoor pit latrine." Since the two words sound so alike in Chewa, the typical person determines from the context whether a person means his latrine or the peak of his hut. In this particular verse, the context wouldn't necessarily make it clear. Doubtless some of the Chewa were not greatly impressed with Satan's challenge that Christ jump off the top of a latrine.[410]

Sometimes tribespeople hearing Scripture for the first time see a fresh humor in it that experienced Bible readers miss. When Jim Loriot translated Christ's parable of the wheat and the tares (Matt 13), the Shipibo listeners thought it was the funniest practical joke they'd ever heard. They laughed out loud as they imagined someone sneaking into a wheat field and planting weeds. They laughed even more when the servants asked the master where the weeds had come from. The Shipibos saw this as self-incriminating, assuming that the servants should have been guarding the fields for their master.

The Shipibos' favorite parable was the story of the Pharisee and the publican (Luke 18). The thought of a pompous old Pharisee walking home with his tail between his legs threw them into peals of laughter. It was not too difficult to see why they found this so hilarious. The Shipibo have a long history of exploitation by landowners and greedy traders who think themselves vastly superior to the Indians.[411]

In our culture, we do not find particularly comical the dilemma the Sadducees posed to Jesus about the woman who married the seven brothers. But when the Gugu-Yalanji Aboriginal people heard the account, they thought it was hysterical. They didn't find preposterous the fact that a man would take his dead brother's wife. That is a tradition in their own culture. What they found humorous was imagining how elderly the woman would be to outlive seven husbands.[412] On the other hand, when some Africans heard this parable,

---

410  Wendland, *The Cultural Factor*, 81.
411  Hefley, *Searchlight on Bible Words*, 150.
412  Ibid., 162.

it seemed incredible that any husband would even want this woman in the resurrection. In their minds, the woman had apparently caused the death of seven husbands by use of witchcraft.[413]

When John and Elaine Beekman translated Scripture into the language of the Chol Indians of southern Mexico, many became Christians. New communities sprang up with such biblical names as Berea, Jerusalem, and Bethlehem. One day Beekman heard of a new village named Egypt. Puzzled about this, he asked why.

"A government official named it," a Chol explained, "probably because there are not many believers there."[414]

An Aborigine language helper read about Matthew who, as a publican, collected money for the government. Assuming the translator had made a mistake, he declared that surely Matthew was *giving* the people money from the government, not taking it. For decades, the Aborigines had been receiving money from the Australian government, so he imagined that every government did the same.[415]

In another case, a language assistant read in Acts 10:44 that "the Holy Ghost fell on all them which heard the word" (KJV). The verb used in his language was the literal word for "fall" in the physical sense. Thus he assumed that the Holy Spirit had tripped in heaven and fallen headlong onto people on earth. It was clear in the passage that no one was hurt, so the assistant concluded that the Spirit must be light in weight if he could fall all the way from heaven and injure no one. The Greek could use the one word "fall" in a spiritual or in a physical sense; this particular language could not.[416]

---

[413] Nida and Reyburn, *Meaning across Cultures*, 73.
[414] Hefley, *Searchlight on Bible Words*, 41.
[415] Beekman and Callow, *Translating the Word of God*, 161.
[416] Ibid., 348.

# Epilogue

# The Nuts and the Bolts

WELL, YOU'VE READ THIS FAR, so maybe the genius of Bible translation has intrigued you, much as it has me. The Bible is not a Middle Eastern relic, nor is it a novelty of the Western world. The gospel is meant to be transferable; it has proven to be the best news ever for all of humanity.

Individuals in every known nation of the world have experienced new birth and spiritual growth in the same way.

So now we touch on the beginnings of Bible translation and then rocket forward to the present and touch on a few crucial matters that linguists wrestle with every day: How is translation work done most efficiently? Are some translations poor and others first class? What is the true balance between stiff literalism and dynamic equivalence? Are functional equivalents vital for scriptural clarity or do they slide dangerously near the heading of linguistic slang? Are the multitude of Bibles written in the cultural simplicity of the "common man" more accurately translations or paraphrases? When does a Bible "translation" step over the line into the realm of adding or subtracting nonnegotiables from the Scriptures?

I'm afraid I don't have definitive answers to all these questions, and it remains an evolving discussion among the great thinkers and theologians who frequent this wondrous world of biblical linguistics.

But, I assure you, they wrestle through these issues with deep reverence, constant prayer, and vigorous thought.

## The Field of Translation

Twenty or thirty pages could easily be devoted to the timeline of Bible books rendered from the original languages of Hebrew, Aramaic, and Greek. Suffice it to say that three of the early translations were the Septuagint (Greek), the Peshitta (Syriac), and the Vulgate (Latin). Also in the fourth century, Ulfilas traveled as a missionary to the Goths in what is now Romania. He devised an alphabet for them and translated the Bible into their tongue. Church historian Kenneth Latourette claims that this was, perhaps, the second known instance of Bible translation. In those early centuries, the Bible was also translated into such languages as Coptic, Armenian, and Ethiopic.[417]

During the Middle Ages, the Bible was translated into the Celtic, Finno-Ugric, Germanic and Turkic families of languages. Roger Bacon did much during this period to purify corrupted texts by emphasizing an intimate knowledge of the original Greek and Hebrew.

In their book, *From One Language to Another*, Nida and Waard explain that when the printing press was invented in the middle of the fifteenth century, there were only thirty-three languages which had anything of the Scriptures, and few of the common people had any access. Such greats as Wycliffe, Tyndale, and Luther attempted to translate and circulate copies of the Scriptures in the vernacular of the people, and they suffered for it. However, by the eighteenth century Roman Catholic missionaries were translating portions of the Bible into various South American languages. By the time the British and Foreign Bible Societies were founded in 1806, portions of the Bible had been translated into approximately eighty languages, and this aided missionaries reaching out to some areas where these were spoken.[418]

During the nineteenth century, some portion of the Bible was translated into about 450 new languages and dialects, over six times

---

[417] Nida and Waard, *One Language to Another*, 195–97.
[418] Ibid., 206, 209.

as many as in the entire period prior to 1800.[419] By the end of 1984, 1,808 languages had at least some portion of the Bible, with 286 languages having the entire book, and 594 the New Testament.[420]

As of this printing, about 4.7 billion people have a Bible available in their first language, and a further 542 million people have at least the New Testament. Current estimates suggest that around 340 million people may still have a need for Bible translation to begin. An expressed goal of translators is that there would be trained and equipped translators working in every language by 2025. Their goal may become easier by reason of language attrition. Some experts claim that by the year 2050, 60–90 percent of the world's approximately seven thousand languages may well be extinct.[421] If you wish to find immediately up-to-date statistics, you may check www.thewordislife.net and click on Scripture Access Statistics.

THE CHALLENGE OF LANGUAGE TRANSLATION

This book has only partially illustrated what an amazingly complex process is language translation. At least three cultures are interacting in every Bible translation: (1) the Hebrew or Greco-Roman cultures, (2) the translator's culture, and (3) the receptor culture. Nowadays, often a translator is also a native speaker, so the translator and receptor may share the same culture. A Bible translator must not only be a linguist, but in many respects an anthropologist. Even this is not enough; translators must also be biblical scholars of a sort, well acquainted with the meticulous work of solid exegesis. They must be able to "draw aside the curtains of linguistic and cultural differences so that people may see clearly the relevance of the original message."[422] Throughout this process, they must also remain intellectually honest and humble. There is, at times, the temptation to "improve" the Bible or slant Scriptures to fit one's own theological convictions. There is also the siren song to introduce highly techni-

---

419 Ibid., 216.
420 Barbara Grimes, email message to author, May 7, 2002.
421 Research based on David Graddol's work and the research of Dr. Luo Qing Chun, Southwest University for Nationalities College of Liberal Arts, Chengdu, China.
422 Nida and Waard, *One Language to Another*, 33.

cal vocabulary or insist on overly literal translation to show off one's knowledge of the original languages.[423]

We may feel that mastering a language such as English is an exceptional accomplishment, but it is evident in this book that even some formerly termed "primitive" languages are, in some aspects, more complicated to translate than English. But because they are not related linguistically to Biblical Hebrew and Koine Greek, translating from the Greek or Hebrew often takes more adjustments than into English. English only utilizes about fifty of the three hundred articulations used in all languages.[424] Zulu has 120 different words simply to describe distinct kinds of walking, and the Malagasy language has words for two hundred kinds of noise and for one hundred separate colors. The Sawi language of eastern Indonesia has nineteen tenses, and concrete verb stems can assume any one of fifteen shapes even before adding suffixes—all these forms indicating whether the action is singular, plural, customary, progressive, repeated, reciprocal, experimental, conclusive, partial, excessive, or obstructed.[425] To add another level of difficulty, in a Quechua language of Bolivia it's possible to take almost any verb root and add over fifty thousand combinations of at least twenty sets of suffixes and particles.[426] And we think English is a challenge!

Some also take pride in the assumption that they understand the theology of the Bible better than most. However, it is evident to translators that some cultures are better suited to understand the Bible because their tribal and clan-oriented cultures more nearly typify biblical Near East cultures than highly technological, individualistic societies. In fact, missiologist Alan Tippett testifies that it was his experience as a missionary to the Fijian people rather than his study of theological tomes or his experience in Western churches that taught him most of what he understands to be sound doctrine regarding the church.[427] And Dom Clements, who served in Ghana, adds several spiritual benefits he received:

---

423 Translation Treasures, *In Other Words*, April–June, 15.
424 Nida, *God's Word*, 16.
425 Richardson, *Peace Child*, 171–72.
426 Kraft, *Christianity in Culture*, 301.
427 Sanneh, *Translating the Message*, 179.

> I think God sent me to Africa . . . that I might learn
> from you some lessons of humility and love and service
> which my rough heart didn't learn in Europe, and you
> Africans whom God has used as tutors to teach me
> these things I thank very much, because even when I
> have been very foolish and said sometimes hateful and
> stupid things to you, you have still gone on in great
> patience . . . And so perhaps in the end I have learned
> some of the things which God sent you to teach me.[428]

Let's quickly review the steps of translation. If translators come in from outside the culture, they must first learn the target language themselves from nationals. Then they must individually identify thousands of words that they have recorded in spoken or written texts in this new language. Next they must decide what these mean and how they correspond to words in their own language. This entails running over multiplied possibilities and making a selection, word for word, from the entire available vocabulary.

We have seen that there are times when translators are unaware of how they're coming across in the particular language. For example, in English we often say "uh" or "ah" every few words, as we struggle to express ourselves. In Mazatec, the word *ah* is the sign of a question. If one says, "The boy went *ah*-school," that means "Was it school the boy went to?" So translators have to be very deliberate in their speech.[429]

The next step is placing the new sounds on paper in a way that is consistent, so that speakers can quickly learn to pronounce their written speech. They must learn that written characters are, in effect, like pictures of the real sounds, words, phrases, and sentences. This must be done: (1) in a manner by which readers have enough information/background to make true sense of what is being said, and (2) in such a manner that readers do not have to work so hard trying to

---

[428] Cited in John Pobee, *The Anglican Story in Ghana: From Mission Beginnings to Province of Ghana* (Accra, Ghana: Amanza, 2006), 159.
[429] Pike, *Words Wanted*, 101.

process the message that their motivation to learn is debilitated or destroyed.[430]

Translators must, at the same time, seek continuously to learn what the Scriptures meant to those who originally wrote and received them. This question constantly haunts the translator. Nida and Waard state: "If we only knew what had prompted certain statements by Paul, it would be so much easier to understand what he was trying to communicate."[431]

Linguists must also decide how formal or informal their translation should be. In English, for example, there are various levels of formality: *The guests may now enter the banquet room; You are invited to dine; Let's go eat now; Let's grab some chow; Soup's on.* If a translation is too formal or wooden, the average person will not be able to understand or identify with it. If it is too informal or loose, the educated classes may view it as not worth their consideration. The word of God must be readily understood just as well by tribal peoples, minorities, factory workers, farmers, and the young, as by business people, radicals, or intellectuals.

When the Gospels and book of Acts were translated into one of the Aymara Indian languages, some language assistants complained about its deadness, suggesting revisions to bring it more into line with the language of villagers. There was strong evidence that "the awkward literalism was the reason why people . . . in the congregation used to go off to sleep during the reading of Scripture." But when the Scripture was adapted to the language of everyday speech, the Aymaras said, "It is as though Jesus Christ were living in our villages."[432]

As recently as the last half of the twentieth century, missionary Bible translation was usually done by two partners with native speakers whom they termed their "national informants." After each book of the Bible was drafted, it was reviewed by both the local speakers and the translators before passing it on to be reviewed meticulously by a visiting consultant. It sometimes had to be typed four or five times

---

430 Freddy Boswell, email message to author, January 2002.
431 Nida and Waard, *One Language to Another*, 15.
432 Nida, *God's Word*, 112, 114.

or more in entirety as the various review stages led to adjustments filling the space between typed lines. Finally a clean copy was needed before it was considered ready for publication. The availability of word processors and relevant computer programs has streamlined the process considerably. Also, speakers of the receptor language who have had some formal education are now given training so that they themselves can produce basic drafts and even edit and update their drafts. Mother tongue speakers tend to translate using comfortable, accurate idioms of their language in place of more stiff, tedious, literal translations that outsiders might produce. Translation is done in teams, with biblical scholars, stylists, resource persons, secretaries, and copy editors, with local speakers doing more and more of the process as they gain experience.

The stylist translates a passage of Scripture, seeking to make it readable (flowing), intelligible (understandable), and acceptable (anticipated) by the receptor audience. Then he or she goes over the chapter verse by verse with a biblical scholar, checking for accuracy and doctrinal consistency. Then the entire local committee reads the draft and discusses possible problems. If the committee reaches an impasse regarding particular problems, these may be referred to an outside consultant. After this, a speaker may read the manuscript to fellow language speakers and ask comprehension questions, marking carefully where reader or listeners stumbled, hesitated, produced wrong forms, or became confused. Finally the manuscript is proofread for form and content by someone who, preferably, has not had earlier connections with the project. Some teams schedule additional rigorous steps to those just mentioned, but this is a general overview of the process.[433]

### Translations: The Good, the Bad, and the Ugly

Totally accurate transference of meaning in translation is impossible. What is in the communicator's mind may be far from what the recipient hears because each comes to the communication event with his or her own assumptions. Put the cross-language factor of translation in there and the level of exact, total transference decreases again.

---

433 Nida and Waard, *One Language to Another*, 202–6.

Many words even spelled alike mean different things in various contexts. A word such as "damn" has quite a different meaning, depending on whether it is uttered in church or on the golf course.[434]

Two speakers of the same language may lose at least twenty percent of intended meaning in a substantive conversation. In the translation of one language to another it is even more difficult to communicate full meaning—some is inevitably lost. Christians are familiar with preachers explaining all the angles of meaning in a particular Greek or Hebrew word, even though it is already translated in the text he read. The area of meaning in any one word of a language never exactly matches the area of meaning for the word used to translate it. The translator's task is to keep such loss at a minimum.[435] Three tests by which translators evaluate themselves are: (1) Is the work so well done that readers might think one of their own people did it? (2) Does the translation smack conspicuously of the translator's views or personality? (3) As much as it is possible to ascertain, does the translation produce in the hearts and minds of readers a similar impression to that produced by the author upon his original readers?[436]

To what extent then should the biblical wording be changed to make it comprehensible in a receptor language? For Bible translators that's the question of the century. There is no easy answer, and a precarious balance must be maintained. If translators develop an unwitting mindset that the Bible must be "improved," this reflects a shallow view of divine revelation. Evangelistic concerns to make the text more readable have also sometimes reflected an underestimation of the spiritual and intellectual capacities of the receptors. On the other hand, translators who attempt to translate the Bible word-for-word into another language have reaped wholesale confusion on the part of readers.[437]

Imagine instructions sent by an American to an Amazonian tribe about where they can find a medicinal root that will stop a murderous epidemic. The American writes: "Start out east of the village and

---

[434] Ibid., 15.
[435] Ibid., 42.
[436] Phillips, *New Testament*, vii.
[437] Nida and Reyburn, *Meaning across Cultures*, 61.

make sure you carry a few small shovels and scrapers. You can take your motorcycle up mountain paths for a few hundred yards, then the undergrowth becomes too thick. With machetes, you'll have to chop your way up another fifty yards or so. On the left side of the mountain, in the grove of trees that appear somewhat like elm, you will find small bulbous-shaped, black roots a few inches beneath the soil. Secure as many of them as possible. When you return to the village, run the roots through an electric grinder, and a bitter-tasting liquid will result. Give about a quarter teaspoon of the liquid to each villager, including those who have not contracted the disease."

Obviously it would be impossible to translate the instructions literally into the Amazonian language. They may have different ways of describing directions such as "east" or "the left side." They probably would not have words for "shovel," "motorcycle," "elm," or "electric grinder." They would not understand measurements such as "yards" and a "quarter teaspoon," etc. These are all items out of another time and culture. Even if the American thought his words so wonderfully written that they must be translated literally, it would be useless, for the local people would comprehend almost none of it. Though this illustration is not ideal, it does show the importance translators must place upon rendering Scripture in terms and concepts each people group can understand.

In view of the challenges, translator Dan Shaw writes:

> It gets very complicated indeed, and I sometimes wonder how we do it, or if it is really possible. Yet this is the task we have set ourselves to and I am impressed with the struggles and the responses. Eventually people will build a theology based on the translation . . . so we must get it right.[438]

Portions of the Bible have been transferred into thousands of languages and dialects. Some Bible translations are excellent; others have proven inferior or sloppily done. Much meaning can be lost to time and inaccuracy, including contemporary allusions and figures of speech, comic expressions religious and artistic dimensions, even

---

438 Dan Shaw, email message to author, November 30, 2001.

basic word meaning. If a translation is culturally foreign or is written with archaic or obscure wording, new readers often assume God is a foreigner, or he must be out of date, or perhaps he has a speech defect.[439] This is an alleged factor in the current King James Version controversies, though multimillions still cherish it.

A quality translation requires a quality commitment of many years. Yet even that translation will not last forever. The rapid increase in worldwide cross-cultural interaction via convenient travel, television, internet, and the mobile phone has brought changes into every language, including English, at an ever-increasing pace. Today, a translation that was published twenty years ago needs revision.

At a translation celebration, a village elder said, "Why has this taken so many years? It is because that word of God says, 'Watch out; be careful so that this work of yours, this unborn child, will not come to a premature birth and die.'"[440]

Some Bible translations are treasured for the memorable wording and remain in use many decades after they are completed; others now languish on shelves or lie hidden in homes or huts because of poor linguistic work. How embarrassing it must have been to a translator when a chief in West Africa prohibited the distribution of a New Testament to his people, saying, "I will not allow our language to be corrupted by the language mistakes in that book."[441]

## Translation, Paraphrase, or Distortion?

The prime function of any form of translation is to express in the target language the main sense of the original Scripture text, plus as much of the subtle nuance as possible without subtracting from the original meaning. As has been said, since language is bound to culture, there will never be a perfect translation which includes both the main sense and every shade or nuance of each verse. However, the attempt to communicate meaning clearly sometimes results in a Bible that is significantly longer than the English Bible. For example, Adoniram Judson translated the Bible into one of the Burmese

---

439 Kraft, *Christianity in Culture*, 263.
440 Shetler, *And the Word Came*, 155.
441 Nida and Waard, *One Language to Another*, 39.

languages of what is now Myanmar. Before printing it, he checked it with Buddhist monks to make sure it was clear and coherent. As a result of their feedback, when the Bible was published it was roughly a third more words than the typical English Bible.[442]

John Beekman states:

> We believe that both the linguistic form and meaning of Scripture are inspired in the original. The Holy Spirit used the linguistic forms of the Hebrew and Greek languages as He found them. To communicate Scripture in another language we must use the linguistic form as we find it. Only in this way can we be faithful to the meaning of Scripture.[443]

While it is true that Bible authors most likely had one primary meaning in mind when they wrote a Scripture, that meaning is not always obvious to us fallible humans two thousand to four thousand years later. The frustration lies in the fact that if translators capture with some precision the *technical* content of a statement, they may sacrifice the *emotional nuances* that form part of the full meaning. And if, in a stroke of genius, they come up with a turn of phrase that conveys powerfully the *message* of the original, the rendering may blur its *factual detail*.[444] This is true for English translations as well as those into other languages.

Translators face a great struggle in making the Bible clear and readable in the receptor language without ending up with a running commentary or an overly loose paraphrase instead of a translation. Some paraphrases can differ significantly from translations. An extreme example is the *Cotton Patch Version* of the New Testament in which Pontius Pilate is governor of Georgia, Annas and Caiaphas are copresidents of the Southern Baptist Convention, and Jesus is born in Gainesville, Georgia, and eventually lynched by an Atlanta mob.[445]

---

442 Larson, *Meaning-based Translation*, 440–41.
443 Hefley, *Searchlight on Bible Words*, 14.
444 Moises Silva, *God, Language, and Scripture: Reading the Bible in the Light of General Linguistics* (Grand Rapids: Zondervan, 1990), 134.
445 Clarence Jordan, *The Cotton Patch Version of Matthew and John* (El Monte, CA: New Win Publishers, 1970).

Though Ken Taylor's *Living Bible* is much more literal than the satirical *Cotton Patch Version*, he made it no secret when he produced it that his work constituted a free translation; that is, more of a paraphrase. His original purpose was to make Scripture alive for his own children; the *New Living Translation* was an attempt to use a clear, everyday English rendering of the original words. He based the work on the original languages but definitely wrote in the common idioms, even slang, of everyday English. However, though he took into account prominent theological interpretations of a verse or passage, he often worded verses in the *Living Bible* in a way that emphasizes one specific interpretation.

We do know the biblical writers intended to be understood, not simply to be admired for their mysticism or the intellectual complexity of their message. Thus Nida and Taber state that "faithful translation involves doing whatever must be done, even including a certain amount of paraphrase," to express the message clearly. They conclude: "Whatever of paraphrase must be included in the translation to make it equivalently intelligible and full of impact, then, is legitimately to be called 'translation' since it is required by the receptor language, not optionally inserted at the whim of the translator."[446]

At the same time, a viable translation attempts, as much as possible, to leave the interpretational options open to the extent that original translations left the options open. Translator Ed Walkwitz states, "If there is a sentence [in Scripture] which has puzzled commentators all the way back to those who were speakers of the Koine Greek, a translator shouldn't rob the reader of the opportunity to consider the questions him- or herself."[447] The *Expositor's Bible Commentary* underlines Walkwitz's point: "In interpreting the sacred text . . . we must beware lest we sacrifice to *clarity* of meaning part of the *fullness* of the meaning." The bottom line is, translators must make the Scriptures clear and accurate without mistranslating

---

[446] Eugene Nida and Charles Taber, *The Theory and Practice of Translation* (Leiden, Netherlands: Brill, 1969), 7–8.
[447] Edward Walkwitz, email message to author, January 2002.

or trying to minutely explain the theological slant of each verse for the reader.

It was a common idea in Bible translation work from the mid-1930s to the early 1970s that if linguists simply (1) translated into cultural idioms, (2) expanded a translation to explain each Scripture in minute detail, and (3) taught the people to read, conversions and spiritual growth would automatically follow.

Now many translators realize that, though it is the Holy Spirit who makes sense of the Bible to the non-Christian, he uses *people* to teach it. It is not possible to translate a New Testament so simply and thoroughly that there will be no need for Bible teachers, especially in explanation and application of more challenging doctrinal and symbolic sections of Scripture. But, of course, if a translation is confusing and obscure because unknown concepts are not clarified somewhere, we cannot assume the Holy Spirit or Bible teachers will somehow clarify the poor linguistic work.

## Different Culture, Different Meanings

This whole discussion of Bible translation inevitably brings up the issue of the inspiration of Scripture. What do evangelical Christians mean when they say the Bible is inspired by God? Traditionally, we mean that the original Scripture manuscripts in their entirety comprise the very words of God to humanity, the authors having been inspired by God's own Spirit as he caused his words to be in the hearts and minds of the writers. Being from God, they are infallible down to the last word. The Bible does not *become* the word of God at certain times, and it does not simply *contain* some words of God within its pages.

Research tells us that, in spite of about twenty centuries of copying the New Testament, only one half of one percent of its content is in question.[448] It is true, however, that even among English translations thousands of words vary from one translation to another, occasionally in significant ways. For example, Fee and Stuart compare four different translations of 1 Corinthians 7:36:

---

448 Josh McDowell, *Evidence that Demands a Verdict: Historical Evidence for the Christian Faith* (San Bernardino, CA: Campus Crusade for Christ, 1972), 51.

"If a man think that he behaveth himself uncomely toward his virgin . . ." (KJV)

"If a man think that he is acting unbecomingly toward his virgin daughter . . ." (NASB)

"If anyone thinks he is acting improperly toward the virgin he is engaged to . . ." (NIV)

"If a man has a partner in celibacy and feels that he is not behaving properly towards her . . ." (NEB)

The KJV leaves the relationship between the man and "his virgin" ambiguous. The NASB renders it a man and his virgin daughter. The NIV interprets the relationship as a man and the virgin to whom he is engaged, while the NEB simply calls the two individuals "partners in celibacy." Fee and Stuart emphasize that none of these is an impossible translation; any of them could conceivably represent what Paul meant with the Greek he wrote. Yet this may be troubling to some. Is one of these translations inspired while the rest are not?[449] Actually, although the Holy Spirit gives guidance to each translation team, we cannot claim that God has chosen one as right in all senses of thought and wording to the exclusion of all others. It is the original text, as just stated, for which we claim inspiration directly from God. All the meanings listed are true and in line with the rest of God's revelation, so one cannot be declared "the best."

As we have said before, contrary to what some may think, when biblical writers penned Scripture, they expressed themselves naturally in Greek and Hebrew idioms. The Greek happened to be Koine—the slangy, ordinary, common people's Greek.[450] These writers were guided by the Spirit, but God also worked through their normal cultural, psychological, and intellectual perspectives and limitations.[451] There is nothing inherently sacred about the languages of Greek and Hebrew. They were the daily languages of those first recipients of Scripture. They are no more perfect or precise than other languages.

---

449 Gordon Fee and Douglas Stuart, *How to Read the Bible for All It's Worth* (Grand Rapids: Zondervan, 1981), 28–29.
450 Charles Kraft, cited in Stott and Coote, *Gospel and Culture*, 298.
451 Kraft, *Christianity in Culture*, 204, 273.

It is the message that is sacred, not the language. The biblical writers did not write to impress, they wrote for understanding.

Nida and Waard state that people have assumed that translation should form a stiff, literal reproduction of the syntactic and lexical features of the source text, even though such renderings may make little sense and may comprise crude distortions of the language being translated. These people fail to realize that the greater the linguistic and cultural distance between the source and the receptor language, the greater the number and extent of the formal changes required to preserve the meaning.[452]

Added to this challenge, Greek and Hebrew words have various shades of meaning or use, as do words in the receptor language. For example, based on linguistic confusion, there have been a number of different renderings of the Hebrew verb form *yahush*, as in Ecclesiastes 2:25. It is rendered "hasten" (KJV), "drink" (NASB), "enjoy" (RSV), and "be anxious" (NEB). And forms of the Greek word *parakaleo/paraklesis* can mean "beseech," "call," "comfort," "console," "exhort," "entreat," "advocate," and more. How does a translator determine which use is inspired by the Holy Spirit?

Also some words change meaning over time. Two of many examples in the English language are the words "ghost" and "spirit," which have actually exchanged meanings. In Elizabethan times, "ghost" meant what "spirit" means today; thus, the archaic biblical rendering, "Holy Ghost." And, conversely, during that period "spirit" meant an apparition or what we call "ghost" today.[453]

Throughout the historical ages, in regard to Bible translation, God has led Bible translators to employ the then-current and natural usage of language in each culture. We should not forget that God's leading or direct command to authors to record his words was expressing spiritual truth in the daily language of the people. Even among English and other major language Bible translations, it is the less strictly literal translations which are by far the most read and readable. There are multitudes of cases in which, when Bible translators stuck tenaciously to the completely literal form or the

---

452 Nida and Waard, *One Language to Another*, 186.
453 Beekman and Callow, *Translating the Word of God*, 346.

base meaning, the results have been wooden, confusing, or outright amusing. For example, the KJV renders Paul as stating literally in Philemon 1:20: "Refresh my bowels in the Lord." That made sense in a past age when a person's deep feelings were described as being in one's bowels. But in a day when the word "bowel" is used primarily in the sense of eliminating bodily waste, and one's deep feelings are described as being in one's heart, isn't it more appropriate to translate with our equivalent idiom "refresh my heart"?

Many Bible translators follow this *dynamic equivalence* approach to translation because they believe it is how God used everyday language to give his Word to the original audiences.[454] The New English Bible committee wrote, "We have conceived our task to be that of understanding the original as precisely as we could, and then saying again in our own idiom what we believed the author to be saying in his. New International Bible translators added:

> [We] have striven for more than a word-for-word translation. Because thought patterns and syntax differ from language to language, faithful communication of the *meaning* of the writers of the Bible demands frequent modification in sentence structure and constant regard for the contextual meaning of words.[455]

This is not a revolving door of empty academic debate and aimless theological wrangling about words. Charles Kraft believes that one reason for the deadness of European Christianity at the popular level is that communicators have become mired in this endless theological tunnel instead of presenting the Bible to the person on the street in language they can understand.[456]

### Have You Dressed the Chicken?

In his quest for proper Bible translation, Eugene Nida, a pioneer of setting out the need for dynamic equivalence, spoke of *formal*

---

[454] Peter Cameron, "Functional Equivalence and the Mot Juste," *Bible Translator* 41, no. 1 (January 1990): 101.
[455] Kenneth Barker, ed., *New International Version Study Bible* (Grand Rapids: Zondervan, 1995), xi.
[456] Kraft, *Christianity in Culture*, 311.

*correspondence* and *functional equivalence*. These big terms have rather simple meanings. *Formal correspondence* means translating the exact Bible words and expressions from the original language into another in the same word order, whether they're intelligible in the receptor language or not. *Functional* or *dynamic equivalence* means translating Bible words, figures of speech, and grammar into equivalents in the receptor language so that they're comprehensible cross-culturally. Nida stated that a translation should stimulate in a reader (in his native language) the same "mood, impression, or reaction that the original writing sought to stimulate in its first readers."[457] Of course, because the original writers are no longer living, they cannot be asked to clarify any wording of which the translator is unsure. Thus, dynamic equivalence is a goal that can only be closely approximated.

"The term functional equivalent or cultural substitution," Tom Pittman states, "sometimes communicates inaccurately what translators do. Great effort is made not to change the original *meaning* of Scripture."

However, as we have seen in this book, one situation in which Bible translators feel justified in moving away from literal translation of the text is when a figure of speech or proper noun is not capable of being understood in a particular culture. For example, some animal and plant-life forms do not exist among a particular people, nor do the people have any context by which to imagine them. Also, constructions such as figures of speech are sometimes peculiar to one language and cannot be understood translated word for word into another. Examples of this abound: "I stepped on the gas," "dress the chicken," "kicking against the pricks," or "It's not a gun that goes off so you can hear it" (meaning "It is very quiet" in Solomon Islands Pijin).[458] Obviously, these would not make sense in another language and culture unless translated using locally equivalent idioms or expressions. Thus, rather than incorporating what would

---

457 Eugene Nida, *Toward a Science of Translating* (Leiden: Brill, 1964), 156, 164.
458 Linda Simons and Hugh Young, *Pijin blong yumi: A Guide to Solomon Islands Pijin* (Honiara, Solomon Islands: Solomon Islands Christian Association, 1979).

be obscure, ambiguous, or confusing expressions into the text of a translation, it seems far better to provide readers with a meaningful equivalent in their language and possible alternatives in the margin, including, if necessary, literal renderings.[459]

This brings up the crucial importance of knowing the target culture as exhaustively as possible. Daniel Shaw, author of *Transculturation*, emphasizes that, when translating, the culture type must be taken into account and how this type interacts with smaller cultural subsystems. If translators misinterpret the customs of the people, they will begin communicating confusing or outright false concepts, either factually, theologically, or regarding the very nature of God. So, while translators are working to make the Scripture completely clear and accurate culturally and semantically in a new language, they are equally determined not to violate the original biblical context and cultural mores.

Linguist George Goolde adds to the discussion. He sees no problem substituting metaphors when absolutely necessary if they are equivalent in function to the biblical metaphors. "For instance," he writes, "'They shall be white as snow,' [Isa 1:18] could have a cultural substitution such as 'They shall be white as egret's feathers.'" This does not do violence to the culture in Isaiah's time because it is an example. It is whiteness being discussed, not snow or feathers as such.

Goolde clarifies that he would not use a cultural substitute where there is a strong doctrinal theme that would be disrupted or distorted in the verse or in other places in Scripture by the substitute. For example, some societies do not have bread, or bread is viewed as expensive "white people's food," looked upon more like a Westerner would view cake. In the Middle East in biblical times, and still today, bread is a staple of every meal. The starch staple in the receptor culture may be sweet potatoes. Still it may not be appropriate to render Christ's claim something like, "I am the sweet potato of life." If there are metaphorical insights about bread in other parts of the Bible that would not hold consistent with sweet potatoes, then the translator should render "bread" with a generic term such as "food" or simply

---

459 Hefley, *Searchlight on Bible Words*, 30, 34.

create a note outside the text to describe adequately to the new culture the importance of bread in Jesus' day and why he claims to be like it.

Another example is the verse in which John the Baptist said, "Look, the Lamb of God who takes away the sin of the world!" (John 1:29). If a group has no idea what a lamb is, this does not mean the translator can render the verse, "Look, the pig of Theos." Though pigs may be common in the given culture, in the Jewish context pigs were anathema, so we would do violence to the original, accurate meaning by this particular change.[460]

However, trying to describe a lamb to a people group that have no earthly clue what it is can also be quite difficult. Should a translator portray John as declaring, "Look, the young, fluffy, white animal shaped somewhat like a dog, which takes away the sin of the world"? It is understandable why translators sometimes avoid attempting to describe an object or concept in this way—it can be laborious and stilted and can bog the reader down, while still perhaps not ensuring that the person will comprehend what is being described. Again, a footnote or glossary item can give the explanatory information. Often a booklet on biblical culture is produced as the translation work proceeds. Thus the people gain understanding without distorting the flow of the text itself.

### WHICH BIBLICAL MODIFICATIONS ARE LEGITIMATE?

What can be equated with the practice of using functional equivalents? The premise of this book is that it is simply a wise way of taking the Scriptures from Middle Eastern or Greco-Roman languages and cultures and deciphering their meaning for totally contrasting cultures.

Most Bible translations don't equate a quality Bible translation with a paraphrase such as the superloose *Letters to Street Christians*,[461] nor with translations which reflect such things as downplaying the existence of hell or judgment, denying the deity of

---

460 George Goolde, email message to author, November 29, 2001.
461 Jack Sparks and Paul Raudenbush, *Letters to Street Christians* (Grand Rapids: Zondervan, 1971).

Christ and the personality of the Holy Spirit, negating the prohibition of homosexuality or the differences between men and women.

Wayne Grudem, ex-president of the Evangelical Theological Society, is quoted as saying, "They state [revisions to various Bible translations] are minimal, but if you change thousands of words that have to do with God and the individual believer, you've changed the tone and emphasis of the whole Bible."[462]

There are at least several significant differences between what conservative Bible translators do in other cultures and what liberal Bible translators are doing in English. First, there is the fact that liberals are attempting to modify theology itself to fit their preconceptions or biases.

Second, liberal translators attempt to turn orthodox Christian conviction on its head by quibbling about minor scriptural examples, which they believe can be twisted to fit their desired interpretations.

Third, conservative translators implement changes in order to make the Scriptures *comprehensible* to a target culture and audience, not to change the meaning of Scripture to something foreign to the original intent.

The fourth point is related to the third. Conservative translators have no choice—they must somehow find a word or idea in the receptor language that is the closest equivalent to the word or phrase in the original text, even if it may seem not precisely synonymous with a word chosen by the translators of a favorite English translation. Their passion is that those in other cultures would understand the Bible just as well in their language and cultural context as we do in our Western world and languages or as the original audience did.

I trust that each time you open your favorite Bible translation you will thank God for translators guided by the Holy Spirit who have struggled long and hard to convey meaningfully God's message.

---

[462] Cited in Eric Gorski, *Sun Sentinel*, Fort Lauderdale, FL, February 2, 2002.

# Bibliography

Allmen, Daniel von. "The Birth of Theology: Contextualization as the Dynamic Element in the Formation of the New Testament." *International Review of Mission* 64, no. 253 (January 1975): 37–55.

Anderson, Neil. *In Search of the Source: A First Encounter with God's Word*. With Hyatt Moore. Portland, OR: Multnomah, 1992.

Bailey, Kenneth. *Poet and Peasant and Through Peasant Eyes: A Literary-cultural Approach to the Parables in Luke*. Grand Rapids: Eerdmans, 1983.

Barker, Kenneth, ed. *New International Version Study Bible*. Grand Rapids: Zondervan, 1995.

Barovick, Harriet. "Tongues that Go out of Style." *Time*, June 10, 2002.

Beekman, John, and John Callow. *Translating the Word of God*. Grand Rapids: Zondervan, 1974.

Cameron, Peter. "Functional Equivalence and the Mot Juste." *Bible Translator* 41, no. 1 (January 1990): 101–9.

Coke, Hugh. *An Ethnohistory of Bible Translation among the Maya*. Ann Arbor: University Microfilms International, 1983.

Evans-Pritchard, Edward. *Theories of Primitive Religion*. London: Oxford University Press, 1965.
Fee, Gordon, and Douglas Stuart. *How to Read the Bible for All It's Worth*. Grand Rapids: Zondervan, 1981.
Fraser, Gordon. *No Dark Valley: A Collection of Stories about Indians and Missions to Indian Tribes*. Flagstaff, AZ: Southwestern School of Missions, 1965.
Frost, Michael. "Translating the Gospel." Centre for Evangelism and Global Mission. http://www.cegm.org (accessed September 26, 2001).
Gorski, Eric. "Gender-neutral Bible Translation Fires Debate Among Evangelicals." *Sun Sentinel*, Fort Lauderdale, FL, February 2, 2002.
Grimes, Barbara. *Ethnologue: Languages of the World*, 14th ed. Dallas: SIL International, 2000.
Guli, John. "The Book of Ruth in Higi." Unpublished manuscript, Fuller Seminary School of World Mission, Pasadena, CA, 1984.
Harjula, Raimo. "Theology as Service in Africa," *Pro Veritate* 11, no. 5 (November 1972): 16–17.
Hefley, James. *Searchlight on Bible Words*. Grand Rapids: Zondervan, 1972.
Hesselgrave, David. *Communicating Christ Cross-culturally*. Grand Rapids: Zondervan, 1978.
Hesselgrave, David, and Edward Rommen. *Contextualization: Meanings, Methods, and Models*. Grand Rapids: Baker Book House, 1989.
*In Other Words*. Translation Treasures. 1972–1978.
Jordan, Clarence. *The Cotton Patch Version of Matthew and John*. El Monte, CA: New Win Publishers, 1970.
Jordan, W. F. *Central American Indians and the Bible*. New York: Revell, 1926.
———. *Glimpses of Indian America: Illustrating Present-day Life in Mexico and Parts of Central and South America*. New York: Revell, 1923.
Koyama, Kosuke. "Thailand: Points of Theological Friction." In *Asian Voices in Christian Theology*, edited by Gerald H. Anderson, 65–86. Maryknoll, NY: Orbis Books, 1976.

Kraft, Charles. *Christianity in Culture*. Maryknoll, NY: Orbis Books, 1979.

Kraft, Charles, and Tom Wisley, eds. *Readings in Dynamic Indigeneity*. Pasadena: William Carey Library, 1979.

Larson, Mildred. *Meaning-based Translation: A Guide to Cross-language Equivalence*. New York: University Press of America, 1984.

Lewis, C. S. *God in the Dock: Essays on Theology and Ethics*. Grand Rapids: Eerdmans, 1970.

Liddell, Henry, and Robert Scott. *A Greek-English Lexicon*. US: Oxford University Press, 1996.

Livingstone, David. *Missionary Travels and Researches in Central Africa*. London: John Murray, 1857.

Loewen, Jacob. "Translating the Names of God: How to Choose the Right Names in the Target Language." *Bible Translator* 36, no. 2 (April 1985): 201–7.

Mason, Francis. *The Karen Apostle*. Boston: Gould & Lincoln, 1861.

Mayers, Marvin. *Christianity Confronts Culture: A Strategy for Cross-cultural Evangelism*. Grand Rapids: Zondervan, 1974.

Mbiti, John. *Concepts of God in Africa*. New York: Praeger, 1970.

McDowell, Josh. *Evidence that Demands a Verdict: Historical Evidence for the Christian Faith*. San Bernardino, CA: Campus Crusade for Christ, 1972.

Moffatt, James. *The New Testament: A New Translation*. Hodder & Stoughton, 1964.

Murphy, Joseph. *Santeria: An African Religion in America*. Boston: Beacon, 1988.

Nida, Eugene. *Bible Translating: An Analysis of Principles and Procedures*. New York: American Bible Society, 1947.

———. *God's Word in Man's Language*. New York: Harper & Row, 1952.

———. *Language Structure and Translation: Essays*. Edited by Anwar Dil. Language Science and National Development. Stanford: Stanford University Press, 1975.

———. *Learning a Foreign Language: A Handbook for Missionaries*. New York: Friendship, 1957.

———. *Toward a Science of Translating.* Leiden: Brill, 1964.
Nida, Eugene, and Charles Taber. *The Theory and Practice of Translation.* Leiden, Netherlands: Brill, 1969.
Nida, Eugene, and Jan de Waard. *From One Language to Another: Functional Equivalence in Bible Translating.* Nashville: Thomas Nelson, 1986.
Nida, Eugene, and William Reyburn. *Meaning across Cultures.* Maryknoll, NY: Orbis Books, 1981.
Olson, Bruce. *Bruchko.* Carol Stream, IL: Creation House, 1978.
Packer, J. I. *Evangelism and the Sovereignty of God.* Chicago: InterVarsity, 1961.
Peters, G. W. "Is Missions Homesteading or Moving?" *Mennonite Herald*, April 15, 1977.
Peterson, Eugene. *The Message: The Bible in Contemporary Language.* Colorado Springs, CO: NavPress, 1995.
Phillips, J. B. *The New Testament in Modern English.* New York: MacMillan, 1958.
Pike, Eunice. *Not Alone.* Chicago: Moody Press, 1956.
———. *An Uttermost Part.* Chicago: Moody Press, 1971.
———. *Words Wanted.* Chicago: Moody Press, 1958.
Pobee, John. *The Anglican Story in Ghana: From Mission Beginnings to Province of Ghana.* Accra, Ghana: Amanza, 2006.
Pride, Kitty. *Bread Is Not Enough.* London: Hodder & Stoughton, 1976.
Reimer, Martha. "It's the Name Above All Names." Unpublished manuscript, n.d.
Reyburn, William. "The Transformation of God and the Conversion of Man." *Practical Anthropology* 4 (1957): 185–94.
Ricard, Robert. *The Spiritual Conquest of Mexico.* Berkeley: University of California Press, 1966.
Richardson, Don. *Eternity in Their Hearts.* Ventura, CA: Regal Books, 1981.
———. *Peace Child.* Glendale, CA: Regal Books, 1974.
Sanneh, Lamin. *Translating the Message: The Missionary Impact on Culture.* Maryknoll, NY: Orbis Books, 1989.

Setiloane, Gabriel. "How the Traditional World-View Persists in the Christianity of the Sotho-Tswana." In *Christianity in Independent Africa*, edited by Edward Fashole-Luke, Richard Gray, Adrian Hastings, and Godwin Tasie, 402–12. Bloomington: Indiana University Press, 1978.

Shaw, Daniel. *Transculturation: The Cultural Factor in Translation and Other Communication Tasks*. Pasadena: William Carey Library, 1988.

Shaw, Mary, ed. *According to Our Ancestors: Folk Texts from Guatemala and Honduras*. Norman, OK: Summer Institute of Linguistics, 1971.

Shetler, Joanne. *And the Word Came with Power*. Orlando: Wycliffe Bible Translators, 2000.

Silva, Moises. *God, Language, and Scripture: Reading the Bible in the Light of General Linguistics*. Grand Rapids: Zondervan, 1990.

Simons, Linda, and Hugh Young. *Pijin blong yumi: A Guide to Solomon Islands Pijin*. Honiara, Solomon Islands: Solomon Islands Christian Association, 1978.

Smith, Edwin. *African Ideas of God*. London: Edinburgh House, 1950.

Sparks, Jack, and Paul Raudenbush. *Letters to Street Christians*. Grand Rapids: Zondervan, 1971.

Steven, Hugh. *They Dared to Be Different*. Irvine, CA: Harvest House, 1976.

Stewart, William A. "Creole Languages in the Caribbean." In *Study of the Role of Foreign Languages in Asia, Africa, and Latin America*, edited by Frank A. Rice, 34–53. Washington DC: Center for Applied Linguistics, 1962.

Stott, John, and Robert Coote, eds. *Gospel and Culture*. Pasadena: William Carey Library, 1979.

Tippett, Alan. *Solomon Islands Christianity*. London: Lutterworth, 1967.

Tucker, Ruth. *From Jerusalem to Irian Jaya: A Biographical History of Christian Missions*. Grand Rapids: Zondervan, 1983.

Wallis, Ethel. *God Speaks Navajo*. New York: Harper & Row, 1968.

Wendland, Ernst. *The Cultural Factor in Bible Translation.* New York: United Bible Societies, 1987.

Wheeler, William, Dwight Day, and James Rodgers. *Modern Missions in Mexico.* Philadelphia: Westminster Press, 1925.

Wilson, Monica. *Religion and the Transformation of Society.* Cambridge: Cambridge University Press, 1971.

# Index

## A

Abel, 107
Aborigine, 77–78, 92, 99, 161
Abraham, 36, 103, 149
Absalom, 156
Adams, Patsy, 21
Africa, 17, 43, 74, 97, 167
    African, 23, 148, 160, 167
        chief, 40
        culture, 63
        language, 33, 101, 103, 112, 148
        myths, 52
        society, 64
Agarabi, 138
Agnew, Arlene, 21
Agtas, 88, 125
Aguacatec, 16
Aguarana, 27, 98–99
Alekano, 29
Ali, Awiame, 131
Alphonse, Efrain, 42
Amahuaca, 29, 31, 82, 110–11, 120
Amazonia
    Amazonian
        language, 171
        tribe, 170
    Lowland, 13
America. *See* United States of America.
Anderson, Lorrie, 105
Anderson, Neilm, 51, 53, 58–60, 64, 78, 81–82, 95, 107, 131, 141–42, 146, 149–51
Andrews, Henrietta, 108
Anglo, 87
animals, 29–30, 39–40, 43, 124, 146, 156
    as illustrations in Scripture, 27
    symbol of, 27
Anuak, 97
Apache, 4, 89
Apollos, 31
Arabelas, 117
Arabic, 18
Aramaic, 164
Armenian, 164
Ashley, Seymour, 156–57
Asia
    Asian, 23
    Southeast. *See* Southeast Asia.

Athens, 36, 94
atonement, 67, 74
Auca, 44
Augustine, 3
Australia, 4, 153
    Australian
    desert, 147
    government, 161
Avokayas, 72
Awa, 13
    language, 13
    people, 13
Aymara, 3, 168
    language, 3, 168
Aztec, 36, 128
    dialect, 112, 128

## B

Babylon, 26
Bacairi, 91
Bacon, Roger, 164
Baer, Mary, 156
Baer, Phillip, 156
Bailey, Kenneth, 55
Bakau, 159
    language, 159
Balangao, 11–12, 109–11
    language, 11
    tribe, 11
Bali, 75
    Balinese, 27, 32, 75, 112
    people, 27
Bamileke
    people, 32
    society, 32
Bangkok, 148
Baptist, 135
    Southern Baptist Convention, 173
Bartimaeus, 151
Batswana, 33
    people, 33
Beekman, Elaine, 161
Beekman, John, 20, 161, 173
Benjamin, 65
Bentley, Bill, 3

Berea, 161
Bethesda, 17
Bethlehem, 161
Bible, 1–3, 8–9, 12–14, 19,
    24–27, 35–37, 41–42, 44, 48,
    51, 56, 59, 69, 87, 107, 109,
    123, 158–59, 163–66, 168,
    170–73, 175, 178–80, 182
    authors, 173
    biblical
    account, 47–48
    attributes, 44
    author, 30
    concepts, 15, 77, 151
    context, 141, 180
    cultures, 23, 26–27, 177, 181
    deity, 36
    expression, 109, 134
    language, 133
    message, 35
    model, 91
    promise, 111
    teaching, 3, 88
    text, 26
    words, 24–25, 54, 103, 134, 137, 139, 170
    writers, 26, 174, 176–77
English, 73, 172–73, 178
Gospel, 8–9, 13, 21, 24, 33,
    35, 38, 45–47, 49, 66, 75,
    81, 85, 104, 154, 163
linguists, 24
readers, 160
Scriptural
    authority, 129
    clarity, 163
    contrast, 83
    repetition, 19
Scripture, 2, 5–6, 8, 11,
    13–14, 16, 18, 21–24, 27,
    37–39, 44, 49, 57, 64, 69,
    74, 78, 83, 90, 101, 106,
    117, 120, 125–27, 130,
    132–35, 137–38, 143, 146,
    154, 160–61, 163–65,
    168–69, 171–76, 179–82

story/stories, 6
students, 76
study, 12, 71, 77, 128
teachers, 175
the Book, 1, 4, 12, 106
translation, 3–4, 13–14, 18, 24, 26, 28, 33, 49, 56, 63, 133, 140, 143, 159, 163–65, 168, 171–72, 175, 175, 177–79, 181–82
  importance of, 4
  King James Version (KJV), 18, 31, 75–76, 100, 126, 140, 142, 144, 154, 156, 161, 172, 176–78
  New International Version (NIV), 17, 176, 178
translator, 1, 3, 14, 25, 35, 71, 78, 81, 87, 133, 153, 165, 170, 177–79, 182
Binumarien Bontoc, 90
  language, 132
  people, 90
Bishop Ruiz, 38
Boaz, 141
Bolivia, 3, 56, 82, 134, 166
Bontoc, 37, 55
  language, 55
  people, 37
Bora, 31, 76, 121
  culture, 158
  language, 72
  people, 158
Borneo, 74
Boxwell, Helen, 154
Boxwell, Maurice, 154
Brant, Albert, 48
Brazil, 29, 91, 101
British and Foreign Bible Societies, 164
Buang, 17, 80
  language, 80
Buddha, 37
Buddhist, 37, 148, 151, 173
Burera, 85, 92
  language, 19, 92

Burgess, Paul, 9
Burma, 48–49
  Burmese, 49, 172
Butler, Jim, 94
Butler, Judy, 94

## C

Cagayan Agta, 72, 88
Cain, 107
Cain, Glen, 48
Cakchiquel, 20
Calcutta, 46
Calvin, John, 3
Cameroon, 43, 55
Canada, 138
  Canadian, 48
Candoshi, 105
  language, 105
cannibalism, 53, 124, 157
Casiguran Agta, 107
celibacy, 176
Celtic, 164
Central Africa, 47, 87, 135
  Central African
    cultures, 88
    Republic, 94
Central America, 29
Chacabo, 56
  language, 56
Chamula
  language, 108
Chatino, 4, 15, 106, 154
  hymns, 106
  language, 15, 154
  people, 4
Chewa, 27, 30, 60, 99, 125–26, 130, 137, 139–43, 160
  culture, 17, 64, 125
  language, 33, 60, 94, 99, 125–26, 137, 139, 142, 160
  people, 139
  society, 75
  translation, 17, 140
Cheyenne, 29
  language, 29

Chiapas, 38
China, 45
   Chinese, 14, 37, 44, 135
   southern, 18
Chinantec Ojitlan, 29, 81, 129, 140
   language, 139
Chitonga
   language, 97
Chols, 15, 56, 125, 155, 161
   language, 81, 137, 155
Chontal, 78, 123
Christian, 1, 6, 8–9, 13, 23, 25, 44, 47, 57, 60, 69, 75, 79–80, 87, 93, 107, 112, 121, 127, 132, 144, 161, 170, 175
   faith, 2, 25, 148
   leadership, 91
   message, 25
   non-Christian, 175
   orthodox, 182
   practice, 25
   song, 7
   theology, 58
   translator, 22
   warrior, 32
Christianity, 103, 107, 178
Christo-paganism, 38, 40
   religious syncretism, 42
Chuj, 126–27
church, 21, 25, 41–42, 45, 48, 54, 99, 131, 134, 158, 164, 166, 170
Clements, Dom, 166
Clevenger, Joy, 93
Cocama, 84
Colombia, 21, 105, 158
Colorado, 129
compassion, 3, 97
Congo, 134
Conob, 97
conversion, 103, 111, 175
Coptic, 164
Cote d'Ivoire (Ivory Coast), 59
Cowan, Florence, 156
Cowan, George, 156
creation, 42, 46, 48, 52

narrative, 143
Cree, 6–7
Creole, 18, 56
Cuicatec, 29, 33, 95, 159
Culina, 21–22
   language, 21
cult, 42
   cultic paraphernalia, 9
culture, 2–3, 11–12, 14, 17, 20, 22–27, 29, 32–33, 35–37, 51, 53, 57–58, 63–65, 80–81, 87–88, 90, 97, 100, 107, 112, 133–34, 138–39, 141, 143–44, 148–50, 155, 158, 160–61, 165–67, 171–72, 175, 177, 179–82
   cultural
      background, 88
      boundaries, 153
      context, 23, 182
      differences, 165
      distance, 177
      equivalent, 54
      heritage, 24
      history, 2
      ideas, 158
      idioms, 112, 175
      language, 23
      patterns, 2
      practice, 14
      simplicity, 163
      status, 57
      substitute, 24, 26–27, 179–80
      traits, 2
   family-centered, 64
   local, 24
   Majority World, 65
   peasant, 55
   visual, 20–21
Cushitic
   language, 136
customs, 24, 26, 64, 68–69, 90, 147, 180

## D

Dahomey, 16
Damascus, 159
David, 158
Davis, Don, 52, 71, 123–24
Davis, Launa, 71
Day of Atonement, 74
de la Torre, Tomas, 37
demon/demonic, 126–28
   idol worship, 135
   possessed, 110, 148
   spirit, 126
Devil. *See* Satan.
Diebler, Ellis, 131, 154
Dumagat
   language, 108
Dyak, 74
dynamic equivalence, 163, 178–79

## E

Earl, Katherine, 120
Earl, Robert, 120
East Africa, 30, 136, 154
Eastman, Bob, 30
Edgerton, Faye, 4
Egypt, 4, 161
elders, 11, 13, 40, 46, 91, 103, 147, 158, 172
Elliot, Ray, 100
Elymas, 29
Engenni, 93
Eskimo, 30, 138
   language, 144
eternal life, 19, 87, 116
Ethiopia, 47
   Ethiopic, 164
Eto, Silas, 41–42
Europe, 167
   European, 23, 178
evangelical, 175
Evangelical Theological Society, 182
Evans, James, 6

evil, 15, 27, 29, 47, 58, 63, 81, 97, 120, 125–29, 151
   spirits, 38, 48, 58, 123, 125–26, 128
exorcism, 8

## F

faith, 9, 13, 18, 20–21, 25, 38, 41, 49, 75, 103–05, 107, 110–13, 124, 142, 148
   Christian. *See* Christian.
family, 6, 59, 63–64, 75, 82, 88, 143–44, 149
   extended, 63
Farnsworth, Marva, 105
Farnsworth, Robin, 105
Fertile Crescent, 2
fidelity
   tension between historical and dynamic, 24
Fiji, 40
   Fijian people, 166
Finland
   Finnish slang, 24
Finno-Ugric, 164
Firchow, Irwin, 57
Firchow, Jackie, 57
Folopa, 51–53, 58–60, 64–65, 76–78, 82, 94–95, 107, 129, 131, 141, 146, 149–51
   culture, 63–64, 107, 141
   language 64, 81, 107
   people, 51
   territory, 59
Fore, 143
   language, 143
forgiveness, 1, 9, 39, 54, 108, 111, 115–16, 118–21
Foris, David, 29, 139–40
Forsberg, Vivian, 112
France
   French, 18
Franklin, Joice, 158
Franklin, Karl, 158
Freiberger, Nancy, 135
Fulani, 100

functional equivalence, 24–26, 30, 33, 38, 138, 163, 179, 181

## G

Gahuku, 154
  people, 154
Gambia, 159
Gedeo, 47–48
genealogy, 12–13
Gerdel, Florence, 127
Germanic, 164
Gethsemane, 73
Ghana, 159, 166
Gibson, Gwen, 85
Glasgow, David, 19, 92
Glasgow, Kathleen, 19, 92
God
  as Creator, 35, 42–48, 51, 53, 57, 150
  as Father, 8, 56–58, 60, 72–73, 79, 89, 154
  holiness of, 56, 85
  names for, 35
    Adonai, 35
    El Elyon, 35
    El Shaddai, 35
    Elohim, 35
    Immanuel, 35
    Jehovah Jireh, 35
  nature of, 42, 51–52, 180
  Yahweh (YHWH), 35
Goddard, Jean, 138
Goolde, George, 180
Gospel. *See* Bible.
grace, 6, 22, 108, 110, 139, 157
Grebe, Karl, 89
Greek, 2, 15, 72, 104, 133, 135, 139, 161, 164, 166, 170, 173–74, 176–77
Green, Diana, 101
Green, Harold, 101
Grimes, Joe, 28
Grudem, Wayne, 182
Guajiro, 100
Guatemala, 14, 20, 94, 100, 126
  Guatemalan, 8

Gugu-Yalanji, 147
  language, 76
  people, 76, 147, 158, 160
Guhu-Samane, 130
  language, 130
Guiaica, 151

## H

Haiti, 18
  Haitian
    Creole, 18
Headland, Tom, 107–08
heart, 8, 33, 41, 43, 45, 60, 67–68, 72, 78, 81, 84, 90, 94, 97–101, 103, 106, 108, 110, 112, 147, 157, 167, 170, 175, 178
Hebrew, 14, 33, 35, 133, 164–66, 170, 173, 176–77
  poetry, 19
Herod, 29, 130
Hershberger, Henry, 76, 158
Hershberger, Ruth, 76, 158
Higi, 141
  culture, 141
Hiligaynon, 19
Hilton, Kenneth, 126
Hinduism
  Hindu, 37, 75
holiness, 16, 93
Holy Spirit, 7, 13, 41, 52, 67, 69, 83, 94, 126–27, 161, 173, 175–77, 181–82
homosexuality, 29, 182
Hooley, Bruce, 80
Hooley, Joyce, 80
hope, 25, 79–80, 112–13, 156
Hopi, 144
  language, 144
Huave, 16
Huichol, 28
  folktales, 28
  language, 28
Hushai, 156

## I

Iduna, 117
  language, 117
Ifugaos, 111
  language, 127
Ila, 43
incantations, 8, 58
India, 2, 46, 115
Inupiat, 30
Iquito, 30, 84
Irian Jaya
  Irian Jayan, 65
Isaiah, 13, 133, 180
Ishmael, 30, 145
Israel, 158
  Israelite, 138, 142
Ixil, 100

## J

Jacob, 25, 65, 142
James, Dorothy, 129
Japan
  Japanese, 15, 18
Jehovah Witness, 41
Jemphrey, Michael, 130–31
Jerusalem, 4, 71, 158, 161
Jesus Christ
  as Savior, 20, 35, 82, 116
  as the Bread of Life, 32
  death, 69, 73, 86, 107, 121, 147
  resurrection, 69, 148, 161
Jewish, 181
  culture, 60, 141
  feast, 138
  people, 35
John the Baptist, 27, 29, 74, 91, 145, 157, 159, 181
Jordan, W. F., 3
Joseph, 32, 65, 141–42
Judah, 65, 140
Judas, 66, 73–74
Judson, Adoniram, 49, 172
Jur Modo, 56, 93, 104

## K

Kaje, 74
  language, 73
Kaka, 43
  language, 155
Kakumasu, James, 120–21
Kakumasu, Kay, 120–21
Kanite, 85
Karanga, 43
Karen, 48–49
Kewa, 158
  language, 158
Kilpatrick, Eileen, 72
King Pachacuti, 45–46
Kingdom of God, 18, 30, 87–91, 93–94, 107
Kipsigis, 119
Kooyer, Martha, 77
Kooyer, Neal, 77
Korea, 45, 135
  Korean, 44–45
Kraft, Charles, 40, 178
Kunjen, 4
  people, 4
Kusai, 159

## L

La Paz, 3
Laban, 142
Lacandon
  people, 156
Lalana, 139
language, 1–2, 4, 6, 8, 11, 13–24, 32, 34, 43, 51–55, 57, 59, 65, 77–78, 82–83, 92, 98, 100, 103–05, 111, 115, 118, 120, 126, 129, 133, 136, 142–45, 147, 150, 153, 155, 159, 161, 164–70, 172–74, 176–80, 182
  assistant, 4, 15, 18, 29, 72–73, 75, 77, 83–84, 88, 90, 100, 121, 132, 161, 168
  dialect, 2, 13, 19–20, 22, 43, 81, 99–101, 108, 110, 112,

120, 128, 156, 159, 164, 171
  direct, 17
  helper, 57, 78, 81, 103, 108–09, 116, 120, 129, 135, 138, 143, 156, 161
  indirect, 17
  local, 133–34
  native, 2, 36, 81, 157, 179
  remote, 101
Larson, Millie, 98–99
Latin, 38, 164
Latourette, Kenneth, 164
Leman, Wayne, 136
Lengua, 90
Liberia, 129
  Liberian, 23, 129
Liddell, 72
Lind, John, 109
linguistic
  challenges, 133
  confusion, 177
  differences, 165
  forms, 173
  journey, 9
  slang, 163
  work, 3, 172, 175
Lisu, 16
Livingstone, David, 36
Loriot, Jim, 111, 145–46, 160
love, 3, 7, 9, 23, 47, 54–57, 67, 75, 77, 81–84, 100–01, 105, 108, 112–13, 115–18, 148, 167
Loving, Aretta, 13
Loving, Richard, 13
Luther, Martin, 3, 164

# M

Machiguenga, 79, 145
  language, 43, 145
Majority World
  cultures, 65
Malagasy
  language, 166
Malawi, 140
Mali, 130–31
Mam
  language, 115
Manambu
  language, 105
Manding, 57
Mangga Buang, 17
Manila, 11
Manobo, 92
  language, 143
  people, 92
  vocabulary, 143
marriage, 64
Marsh, James, 4
Mary, 36, 148, 155
Mastra, Wayan, 75
Maxakali, 29
Mayan, 38, 115
  culture, 38
  god, 37
  language, 38, 97
  people, 37
Mayfield, Georgialee, 72, 88, 124–25
Mayfield, Roy, 72, 88, 124–25
Mazahua, 103, 159
  language, 103
Mazatec, 6, 8, 20, 22, 37, 40, 60–61, 73, 83–84, 104–05, 111, 125, 127, 140, 144, 156–57, 167
  language, 83, 140
  people, 110
Mbaka, 47
McCarthy, Joy, 85
Melanesia, 54
  Melanesian society, 57–58
Melchizedek, 36
Mesquital Valley, 1
Mexico, 1–2, 4, 15, 17, 28–29, 37, 64, 78, 81, 95, 99, 101, 103, 108, 119–20, 125–26, 139, 156, 161
  Mexican, 81
    languages, 129
    marketplace, 5
Mid-Waria Agta, 86

language, 85
Middle East, 33, 180
　Middle Eastern(er), 54
　　expression, 155
　　funeral, 149
　　language, 145, 181
　　relic, 163
mission, 41
　work, 37–38
missionary, 5–7, 9, 23, 25, 36, 38–42, 44–46, 48–49, 55, 57, 65, 87, 123, 134, 138, 154, 164, 166, 168
　school, 49, 109
Mixe
　language, 17
Mixteco, 20, 101
Mormon, 41
Moses, 158
Mossi
　people, 53
Motilone, 21
Mount Golgotha, 75
Mount Harata, 46
Mud Sea, 4
Muinane, 73, 90
　culture, 73
　language, 90
Mukuchua, 77
Muong, 143
Muyuw, 31
Myanmar, 173

# N

Naomi, 17, 141
Navajo, 4, 60, 89, 144, 150
　language, 89
Ndonga
　language, 128–129
Near East
　cultures, 166
New Hebrides, 88
New Testament, 1, 12, 23, 54, 80, 85, 98, 111, 121, 124, 130, 165, 172–73, 175
Nicodemus, 108

Nida, Eugene, 36, 140, 164, 168, 174, 177–79
Noah, 14
Nogo, 4–5
North America, 42
Nsoq, 89
　culture, 89
　palace, 89
Nung, 135
　language, 136
Nushu
　language, 18

# O

Oatridge, Desmond, 90, 132
Oatridge, Jennifer, 90
Ojitlan, 81
Old Testament, 74–75, 89, 145, 149
Olson, Bruce, 21
Orejon, 84, 91
　language, 91
Orizaba Nawati, 56
Oro Sin, 13
Otomi, 1, 29, 33, 108, 119

# P

Packer, J. I., 33
Paez, 105
　language, 105
Palikur, 101
Palistine, 75, 142
Pame, 29
Papua New Guinea, 13, 31, 51, 54, 63, 85, 104, 106, 117, 119, 129, 154, 158
　Eastern Highlands, 143
parable, 55, 92, 143, 146, 148, 156, 160
Paraguay, 90
Passover, 137–38
Paul, 16, 18, 29, 32, 36, 43, 54, 64–65, 75, 80–81, 88, 90, 93–95, 98–99, 109, 111–12,

119, 130–31, 134, 142, 155,
    158–59, 168, 176, 178
Pawnee, 42
peace, 66–67, 69, 81, 85–86, 88,
    101, 112, 116, 158
Peck, Dudley, 115
Peeke, Catherine, 57
Pentecost, 16
people groups, 2, 45, 77, 125,
    171, 181
Persson, Andrew, 104
Peru, 5, 21, 31, 76, 79, 91, 98,
    100, 105, 111, 117, 121, 145,
    158
    Peruvian, 121, 139
        language, 143
Peshitta, 164
Peter, 16, 31, 73, 90, 119, 123–24
Pharisees, 101, 130, 136, 139,
    147, 160
Philippines, 11, 19, 37, 88, 107,
    112, 127, 130, 137, 143, 148
    Filipino, 92, 124, 135, 143,
        156–57
Phillips, J. B., 26
Pike, Eunice, 3, 6, 8, 37, 73, 83,
    125, 128
Piro
    language, 111
Pitjantjatjara
    language, 153
Pittman, Tom, 179
Plateria, 5
polygamy, 25
Polynesia, 54
pornography
    pornographic literature, 18
Potiphar
    wife, 141–42
prayer, 9, 12, 42, 57–58, 60, 150,
    164
Pride, Kitty, 4, 15, 106, 154
Pride, Leslie, 4, 15, 154
Priest, Anne, 82
Priest, Perry, 82, 116–17, 121
Prost, Gilbert, 56
Prost, Marian, 56

prostitute, 30, 140–41
Protestant, 45
Punuyaba, 13
Putumayo River, 158

## Q

Quechua, 3, 134
    language, 166
Quiche
    language, 14

## R

Rachel, 142
Rangoon, 48–49
reconciliation, 55, 63, 86
reflective digestion, 26
Reid, Lawrence, 37, 55
religion, 94
    folk, 45
    foreign, 24
    religious, 2, 94–95, 171
    world, 75
Reuben, 135
rhetorical
    devices, 19
    questions, 18
Ricci, Matthew, 36
Rich, Furne, 117–18
Rich, Rolland, 117
Richardson, Don, 45, 65–69
Richert, Ernest, 85–86, 130
Richert, Marjorie, 85–86, 130
Rincon, 99, 110, 120
Roberts, Oral, 41
Roman Catholic, 37–38, 42, 164
Romania, 164
Rosenau, Ferdinand, 47
Rotokas, 57
Russia
    Russian coast, 13
Ruth, 17, 64, 137, 141

## S

sacrifice, 39, 46–47, 63, 66,
    74–75, 94, 138, 150, 173–74

Sadducees, 160
Sahara, 53
Saint, Rachel, 44, 57, 101, 110
salvation, 3, 38–39, 108–09, 112–13
Samaritan, 146, 148
Samo, 53, 112–13, 136
    language, 115, 136
    people, 54
Sanhedrin, 150
Santa Maria, 8
Santal, 46
    people, 46–47
Satan, 21, 46, 48, 52, 123–27, 131, 160
    Devil, 29, 39, 43, 123, 127
Saul, 140
Sawi, 65–69
    language, 166
Schmidt, Wilhelm, 45
Scott, Graham, 72, 143–44
Scott, Margaret, 143–44
Scripture. *See* Bible.
Sea of Blood, 4
Sea of Pitch, 4
Septuagint, 164
sex, 116
    opposite, 129
    sexual
        immorality, 16
        relations, 148
Shaw, Dan, 53, 141, 171
Shetler, Joanne, 11–12, 109–11
Shilluk, 99, 119
Shipibo, 111, 139, 160
    language, 100, 111
Shona
    people, 43
Siane
    language, 129
Sidon, 26
Sierra Juarez, 134
Sierra Popoluca, 109
sin, 7, 14–15, 17, 26, 40, 44, 52–53, 74–76, 85, 99, 107, 109–11, 116, 118–19, 121, 124, 129–32, 141, 155, 181

Singh, Bakht, 115–16
Siriono, 82–83, 116, 121
    language, 82, 116, 121
Skrefsrud, Lars, 46–47
Slocum, Marianna, 3, 105, 127
Smith, Paul, 81
Snell, Betty, 43, 79, 145
Snell, Wayne, 43, 79, 145
Sochiapan, 29, 140
Solomon Island ghost cult, 42
South Africa, 33, 129
South America, 100, 157
    South American language, 164
South Korea, 45
Southeast Asia, 16, 31
Spaniards, 46
Spanish, 1–2, 8, 37, 83, 105, 139–40, 159
spiritual
    benefits, 166
    confession, 38
    fruit, 92
    fulfillment, 45
    growth, 163, 175
    harvest, 49
    house, 54
    knowledge, 4
    life, 124
    maturity, 9, 111
    meaning, 85
    need, 32
    phenomena, 41
    powers, 25
    purpose, 91
    significance, 109
    soldier, 32
    truth, 177
    victory, 93
Spotts, Hazel, 103
St. Lucian Creole, 56
Stringer, Mary, 119
Sudan, 72, 99, 155
    southern, 56, 104
    Sudanese, 99
Suena, 104
    language, 104

Supyire, 131
   language, 130
Swahili, 93
Swick, Ron, 118
Syria, 158
Syriac, 164

## T

*ta ethne*, 2
Tagabili, 130
   people, 112
Tango
   Tangoan language, 88
Tarahumara, 126
Tausug, 157
   language, 156–57
Tavexicua, 28
Taylor, Ken, 174
temptation, 15, 49, 129, 132, 160, 165
Tetelcingo Nahuatl, 56
Teutilo, 29
Thailand
   Thai, 148
      congregation, 148
theology, 25, 58, 166, 171, 182
Thiesen, Eva, 76
Thiesen, Wesley, 72, 76
Thomas, Elaine, 93
Tila Chol, 56
Timorese, 118
Tippett, A. R., 41, 166
Tobiona, 13
Tonga, 17, 27, 30–31, 53, 97, 142, 156, 158
   culture, 30, 64, 139
   language, 52, 65, 94, 97, 135
Toura, 59
   language, 58
translation, 25–26, 57–58, 60, 64, 71, 73, 75–76, 84, 98–99, 118, 124, 139–40, 142, 145, 154, 156, 163–64, 167–82
   assistants/helper, 13, 80, 82, 86, 104–06, 140, 144
   Bible translation. *See* Bible.
   completion of, 19
   correct, 99
   dream, 3
   literal, 166, 169, 179
   process of, 9, 100
   projects, 134
   quandary, 91
   team, 13
   work, 6, 116, 153
translator, 1, 3, 5–6, 8, 13–19, 23–27, 29–31, 34–38, 41, 51–54, 56, 58–59, 61, 64–65, 71, 73, 75–80, 84–85, 87–89, 91–93, 95, 98–99, 103–08, 110–12, 117–21, 126–30, 133–41, 143–45, 147–50, 153–59, 161, 165–68, 170–75, 177, 179–82
   Bible. *See* Bible.
   Christian. *See* Christian.
Trinity, 41, 45
Trique, 18, 129, 139
   language, 18
trust, 25, 75, 77, 82, 103, 105, 107, 111–12
truth, 4–5, 23, 33, 39, 41–42, 46–47, 49, 52, 68, 101, 112, 127, 134, 136, 139, 157–58, 177
Tsonga, 33, 129
Tumbukas, 140
Turkey
   Turkic, 164
   Turkish language, 125
Twi, 17
Tyndale, 164
Tyre, 26
Tzeltal, 3, 64, 127
   language, 3, 112
Tzutujil, 94
   language, 94

## U

Uduk, 98, 155
United States of America, 3–4
   American, 170–71

soldiers, 42
Urubu, 98, 120
Usarufa
  language, 5

## V

Valiente, 42, 80, 91, 112
Velasquez, Marcelino, 9
Velie, Dan, 91
Velie, Virginia, 91
Venezuela, 151
Vietnam, 143
  Vietnamese, 135, 137
Villa Alta, 29
violence, 65–66, 77, 180–81
Vishnu, 37
Votic
  language, 13
Vulgate, 164

## W

Waard, John de, 164, 168, 177
Waffa, 119–20
Walkwitz, Ed, 174
Wange, Warrasa, 47–48
Wantoat, 71, 123–24
  language, 52, 71, 85
Waorani, 57, 98, 101, 110, 157
  language, 44, 110
Washkuk, 77
  language, 77
  people group, 77
Weri, 154
Welsey, John, 41
West Africa, 16, 109, 148, 155, 172
  West African, 33
Western, 95
  churches, 166
  culture, 24
    industrialized, 23
  hemisphere, 28
  mind, 87
  mindset, 21
  nations, 87

Westerners, 55, 63, 73, 77, 120, 159, 180
world, 2, 163, 182
witch doctors, 8–9, 91, 127
witchcraft, 1, 21, 25, 127, 161
worship, 25, 37, 41, 45–46, 56, 94–95, 135, 150, 159
Wrigglesworth, Hazel, 92
Wycliffe Bible Translator, 120, 164

## X

Xhosa, 42, 53
  people, 42

## Y

Yagua, 84
Yakima, 42
Yamba, 155
Yaweyuha
  people, 131

## Z

Zaccheus, 3
Zambia, 30, 43, 64, 97
Zanaki, 31–32
  people, 31
Zapotec, 110, 120, 134
  language, 16
  people, 99
Zapotes, 29
Zimbabwe, 31
Zulu, 44, 166
  people, 44

# Scripture Index

Genesis 1, 51
Genesis 1:2, 52
Genesis 2:24, 64
Genesis 3:19, 141
Genesis 4:10, 107
Genesis 4:10–11, 107
Genesis 9, 53
Genesis 14:18–20, 36
Genesis 15:1, 154
Genesis 16:12, 30
Genesis 31:35, 143
Genesis 38:15, 140
Leviticus 16, 74
Judges 21:25, 129
Ruth 2:7, 137
Ruth 2:18, 64
2 Samuel 10, 158
2 Samuel 16:16, 156
2 Chronicles 20:21, 16
Job 13:12, 139
Job 33:20, 99
Job 39:15, 32
Psalm 23, 126
Psalm 30:11, 32
Psalm 75:10, 125
Psalm 89:17, 24, 125
Ecclesiastes 2:25, 177

Ecclesiastes 3:11, 45
Song of Solomon 1:2, 30
Song of Solomon 4:15, 31
Isaiah 1:18, 180
Isaiah 55:11, 13

Matthew 3:7, 27
Matthew 3:11, 32
Matthew 4:5, 160
Matthew 5:13, 92
Matthew 6, 98, 154
Matthew 6:13, 129
Matthew 7:15, 29
Matthew 7:28–29, 90
Matthew 9:5, 118
Matthew 9:23, 149
Matthew 10, 27
Matthew 11:21, 26
Matthew 11:28, 60
Matthew 11:29, 61
Matthew 13, 160
Matthew 15:32, 97
Matthew 16:16, 90
Matthew 18:21, 119
Matthew 20:21, 17
Matthew 21, 156
Matthew 27:32, 75

Mark 1:3, 133
Mark 1:6, 144
Mark 1:15, 154
Mark 1:41, 127
Mark 2:11, 159
Mark 2:22, 32
Mark 3:5, 101
Mark 3:27, 131
Mark 4:17, 137
Mark 4:20, 92
Mark 4:30, 18
Mark 5:35, 17
Mark 5:36, 105
Mark 6, 98
Mark 6:20, 91
Mark 8, 135
Mark 8:15, 130
Mark 9:23, 105
Mark 9:31, 78
Mark 10:13, 127
Mark 10:31, 143
Mark 10:35, 30
Mark 10:37, 89
Mark 12:38, 40, 156
Mark 14:1, 98, 138
Mark 14:36, 57
Mark 14:63, 15
Mark 16:14, 100
Luke 1:41, 145
Luke 3:7, 27
Luke 4:9, 160
Luke 5:39, 136
Luke 6:27, 35, 117
Luke 6:44, 32
Luke 8, 92
Luke 8:49, 17
Luke 9:58, 17
Luke 11:11, 59
Luke 12:54–55, 142
Luke 14:26, 149
Luke 15:8–10, 143
Luke 15:11, 154
Luke 18, 160
Luke 18:13, 33
Luke 23:34, 139
Luke 24:32, 99
John 1:1, 72–73, 157

John 1:12, 108
John 1:14, 157
John 1:17, 139
John 1:29, 74, 181
John 3, 8
John 3:3, 88
John 3:16, 67, 81–84
John 3:17, 109–10
John 5:14, 17
John 6, 136
John 6:47, 153
John 8:12, 16
John 8:44, 124
John 10:9, 31
John 10:12, 29
John 11:14, 139
John 13:23; 19:26; 21:7, 20, 17
John 14:1, 98, 106
John 15:7, 59
John 18:6, 73
John 18:11, 73
John 20:25, 148
Acts 2:15, 16
Acts 2:34–35, 89
Acts 4:31, 127
Acts 5:41, 150
Acts 8:9–24, 127
Acts 10:44, 161
Acts 12:13, 31
Acts 13:10, 29
Acts 14:8, 140
Acts 15:10, 137
Acts 16:31, 104
Acts 17:22, 94
Acts 17:23, 95
Acts 17:27, 43
Acts 20:37, 158
Romans 3:17, 81
Romans 4, 103
Romans 7:24, 65
Romans 12:1, 128
Romans 12:20, 134
Romans 14:2, 142
1 Corinthians 3:5, 18
1 Corinthians 3:6, 31
1 Corinthians 5:6–7, 131
1 Corinthians 7:36, 175

1 Corinthians 9:5, 155
1 Corinthians 14:9, 134
Galatians 5:9, 130
Ephesians 2:8, 110
Ephesians 2:14, 85
Philippians 4:13, 16
Colossians 1:18, 98
1 Thessalonians 2:18, 93
1 Thessalonians 5:8–9, 112
1 Thessalonians 5:21, 144
1 Timothy 1:15, 112
2 Timothy 2:4, 32
2 Timothy 2:17, 144
Philemon 1:20, 178
Hebrews 1:8, 90
Hebrews 6:19, 26, 53
Hebrews 9:4, 144
Hebrews 9:12, 85
James 3:6, 137
James 3:11, 156
James 3:12, 27
James 5:14, 158
1 Peter 5:7, 60
1 Peter 5:8, 123–24
1 Peter 5:8–9, 21
1 John, 8, 13, 56, 121
1 John 3:1, 56
1 John 3:14, 84
1 John 4:11, 116
1 John 5:6, 76
2 John 13
Revelation 3:20, 31–32
Revelation 13:15, 154
Revelation 18:19, 26